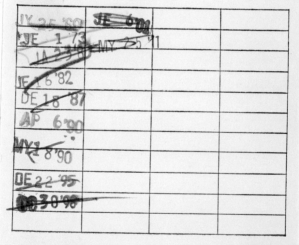

Date Due

JY 25 '80	JE 6 '02		
JE 1 '73			
JA 3 '75	MY 25 '11		
JE 16 '82			
DE 16 '87			
AP 6 '90			
MY 18 '90			
DE 22 '95			
DE 30 '98			

Carl R. Proffer

KEYS TO LOLITA

Bloomington

INDIANA UNIVERSITY PRESS

London

for Ellendea

FOREWORD

This is not an "interpretation" of *Lolita*. Except in a purely incidental way I have not concerned myself with the character of the hero or the heroine, the meaning or morality of the novel, believing that anyone who has read the book carefully will understand these generalities, and that, in any case, after Nabokov's own lucid narrative any paraphrase would be more reprehensible than raping Mabel Glave. What I offer are keys to some of the technical puzzles—isolation, labeling, and commentary on the literary allusions, an inventory of the clues and deductions leading to Quilty's identity, and a listing of some characteristic stylistic devices. This exegetical exercise in close reading is proffered as an introduction to the realms hidden in Nabokov's secretly sliding panels and double-bottomed drawers. Because it is important to have a fresh impression of how badly one may be deceived, the more recently my reader has read *Lolita*, the more comprehensible and useful this book will be. A final word: some may say my commentary is a parody of Nabokov. This, of course, is probably untrue.

July 15–November 24, 1966
PORTLAND–BLOOMINGTON

ACKNOWLEDGEMENTS

My thanks to Ed Baker, H. D. Cameron, C. Grier Davis, John Houston, Mona Houston, and Sidney Monas for their allusive assistance.

For his expert suggestions, my special gratitude to Mark V. Boldino.

CONTENTS

Foreword   vii

Chapter

ONE   LITERARY ALLUSION   3

TWO   IN QUEST OF QUIMBY-QUIX-QUILTY   57

THREE   STYLE   81

Appendix A Characteristic Imagery   121

Appendix B A Calendar of *Lolita*   125

Notes   131

Index   155

Tum-tee-tum. And once more—TUM! I have not gone mad. I am merely producing gleeful little sounds. The kind of glee one experiences upon making an April fool of someone. And a damned good fool I *have* made of someone. Who is he? Gentle reader, look at yourself in the mirror.

Despair

ONE ▎▎ LITERARY ALLUSION

The learned reader must have observed that in the course of this mighty work I have often translated passages out of the best ancient authors without quoting the original or without taking the least notice of the book from which they are borrowed.

TOM JONES

Chapter One

$\llcorner$OLITA was suggested to Vladimir Nabokov by Boris Ivanovich Shchyogolev, a not particularly intelligent character in one of his Russian novels *(Dar)* written in the years 1934-37. The apposite passage goes like this:

"Ah, if only I had a tick or two, *what a novel* I'd whip off! From real life. Imagine this kind of thing: an old dog—but still in his prime, fiery, thirsting for happiness—gets to know a widow, and she has a daughter, still quite a little girl—you know what I mean—when nothing is formed yet but already she has a way of walking that drives you out of your mind—A slip of a girl, very fair, pale, with blue under the eyes—and of course she doesn't even look at the old goat. What to do? Well, not long thinking, he ups and marries the widow. Okay. They settle down the three of them. Here you can go on indefinitely—the temptation, the eternal torment, the itch, the mad hopes. And the upshot—a miscalculation. Time flies, he gets older, she blossoms out—and not a sausage. Just walks by and scorches you with a look of contempt. Eh? D'you feel here a kind of Dostoevskian tragedy? That story, you see, happened to a great friend of mine, once upon a time in fairyland when Old King Cole was a merry old soul," and Boris Ivanovich, turning his dark eyes away, pursed his lips and emitted a melancholy, bursting sound.[1]

3

Because of Boris and the Dostoevskian tragedy, I find
Nabokov's own eccentric account of the genesis of his best
novel just a little misleading. He writes:

The first little throb of *Lolita* went through me late in 1939
or early in 1940, in Paris, at a time when I was laid up with a
severe attack of intercostal neuralgia. As far as I can recall, the
initial shiver of inspiration was somehow prompted by a newspaper story about an ape in the Jardin des Plantes . . .[2]

Of course, it really doesn't matter what the truth is; and
the real Nabokov has a perfect right to create a fictitious
Nabokov if he wants to. My point is that one should always
be suspicious, because casual and credulous readers will
share the fate of Nabokov's butterflies.

Another typically Nabokovian piece of tomfoolery occurs
in another recent foreword to a translated novel: "My
favorite author (1768–1849) once said of a novel now utterly
forgotten *Il a tout pour tous* . . ."[3] He doesn't explain who
the author is or what he was writing about. How does one
figure out who Nabokov's favorite author is with nothing
to go on but a quote about a forgotten novel and two dates
—one of which, as it turns out, is wrong? Well, this author
is probably, though not necessarily, French; with a little
stubborn research and some help from remarks in Nabokov's
Commentary on *Eugene Onegin* ["*René*, a work of genius
by the greatest French writer of his time . . ." (*Eugene
Onegin*, Commentary, Vol. III, p. 98)] the answer turns
out to be François (Auguste) René, Vicomte de Chateaubriand (1768–1848), whose death date is given accurately
in the *Onegin* Commentary. What does all this prove?
Nothing—except that anyone who is going to read a somewhat sadistic author like Nabokov must keep encyclopedias,

dictionaries, and handbooks handy if he wants to understand even half of what is going on (I didn't disentomb the forgotten novel). This is rather annoying because works of art can have more wit than does them good—but literary puzzles are sometimes diverting. The reader must be a researcher.[4]

My third introductory point can be illustrated by a passage from *The Defense*, Nabokov's novel about the poor, brilliant chess player, Luzhin. One evening Mrs. Luzhin finally manages to get rid of some guests and: ". . . quickly embracing her husband, she began to kiss him—on the right eye, then the chin, then the left ear—observing a strict sequence that had once been approved by him."[5] At this point in the story Luzhin's compassionate wife, one of the warmest of Nabokov's creations, has been doing everything possible to prevent him from thinking about chess, because his monomania had already led to a serious breakdown. For all her solicitude she does not see—but, subliminally, he does—that the line described by this queer osculatory sequence is a perfect imitation of a knight's move. This is typical of the detail used by Nabokov. Everything has a meaning; connections hide just beneath the surface. The reader must move slowly—and think logically.

Few writers require more of their audience than Nabokov. This study is dedicated to showing some of the tasks one must perform in the course of a slow, suspicious, thoughtful consideration of the details. The evidence presented suggests that the ideal reader of *Lolita* would be a literary scholar trained and widely read in several European languages, a Sherlock Holmes, a first-rate poet, and the possessor of an eidetic memory.

2

Before proceeding to the large subject of literary allusion
in *Lolita,* I would like to give a few illustrations of the kinds
of details which must be remembered and connections
which must be made if one is to enjoy those stabs of esthetic
ecstasy and recognition which Nabokov so carefully prepares. For example, Humbert reports that when he drove
up to the Haze house for the very first time he "almost ran
over a meddlesome suburban dog (one of those who lie in
wait for cars)" (p. 38). An unimportant detail? No—the
meddlesome Junk dog is one of the intricacies of Nabokov's
pattern. Several months (and many pages) later, it is to
avoid hitting this same dog that Fred Beale swerves his
car, crushing Charlotte Haze precisely at the moment of
Humbert's apparent undoing; fortunes are reversed, and
Humbert becomes the sole guardian and master of Lolita.
For want of that dog, Lo would have been lost.

Another example. When Humbert arrives at Camp Q.
to pick up Lolita, he is pointed to the Camp Director by a
sullen "redheaded impish lad" (p. 112), whose name, we
learn in passing, is Charlie. As Humbert leaves with Lolita,
he says to himself, "Good-bye, Camp Q., merry Camp Q.
Good-bye, plain unwholesome food, good-bye Charlie"
(p. 113). That same night Humbert possesses Lolita for the
first time. But she confesses that she and her friend Barbara
had often rowed to an island and taken turns "doing it"
with, in Humbert's words, "the silent, coarse and surly but
indefatigable Charlie" (p. 139). Thus we learn that Humbert has unknowingly confronted Lolita's first violator. But
what is even more amusing and ghastly is a conclusion

which Humbert himself does not make at the time. Humbert records, without comment, that when he and Lo drove away from camp: "She had had a long long day, she had gone rowing with Barbara . . . and had been active in other ways too" (p. 124). If the reader remembers this sentence when, twenty pages later, he reads the "confession" about Charlie Holmes, he can make an interesting deduction: Lo was behind the bushes with Charlie that morning, and in bed with Humbert that night—a grotesque double duty of which jealous Humbert remains mercifully unaware.

If we jump from the first to the last day of Humbert's control of Lola, we find another example of authorial irony and the necessity for close reading. Humbert is in a nearby motel when Quilty checks Lolita out of the Elphinstone hospital just after two o'clock. The date can be deduced. That very day as Humbert lay ill: ". . . there was some great national celebration in town judging by the firecrackers, veritable bombs, that exploded all the time . . ." (p. 247). At five minutes to two he receives a solicitous phone call from the hospital; he assures the nurse he won't visit until the next day. But the next day he learns that Lolita had checked out of the hospital—and his life—just after two o'clock. In the next chapter, buried not too obtrusively in a passage describing Humbert's itinerary for June and July, he notes that Lo and he had reached Elphinstone "about a week before Independence Day" (p. 249). Quilty, with a Nabokovian sense of irony, had contrived to liberate Lolita from Humbert on the Fourth of July. But lucky Humbert does not make the connection and is spared the cruel wit.[6]

One final example of Nabokov's use of detail, his repetition of certain themes, can serve as a bridge to the discussion of literary allusions. Nabokov says ("On a Book Entitled

Lolita") the class list of Ramsdale School (pp. 53–54) is one
of the passages he always remembers with special delectation.[7] About half of the names do occur at various points
later in the novel. For example, one of the girls is "Fantazia,
Stella." Humbert refers to her as "adorable Stella, who has
let strangers touch her" (p. 55). Like so many of the characters mentioned, she refuses to die after an initial fleeting
appearance. Near the very end of *Lolita,* when Humbert
returns to Ramsdale in quest of Quilty, he enters the hotel
barroom where years before he had conquered Charlotte's
heart with a half-bottle of champagne. The class-list reverberates in a name and an adjective:

As then, a moon-faced waiter was arranging with stellar care
fifty sherries on a round tray for a wedding party. Murphy-
Fantasia, this time. [p. 291][8]

"Fantazia, Stella" appears, after an interval of over fifty
chapters, as "stellar . . . Fantasia." Presumably, Nabokov
feels that anyone who realizes why the waiter arranges the
sherries with "stellar" care will be amply rewarded. He
should, Nabokov might say, feel the keen delight of being
a chess player, and pride and relief, and the psysiological
sense of harmony which is so well known to artists.

3

Nabokov takes particular pleasure in playing with
names.[9] The memoirist's name is an inspired choice. It
undergoes various transformations, distortions, additions,
and modifications—determined by a perfect interfusion of
phonetics, sense, and literary allusion. Here are some of
the guises in which Humbert appears:

Humbert the Terrible, Humbert the Small, Humbert the Wounded Spider, Humbert the Hoarse, Humbert the Humble, Humbert the Hound, Humbert the Cubus, Humbert le Bel, Humbert the Hummer, Humbert the popular butcher, Herr Humbert, Humbertoldi, Jean-Jacques Humbert, San Humbertino Humbert, Homburg, Hamburg, Humbug, Humbird, Humburg, Hummerson, Hummer.

And in a similar vein we find:

Humbert Humbert lumbering, Hum and Mum, Hummy and Mummy, umber and Humberland, a Hamburger and a Humburger, the humble hunchback.

Following an erection he has to "shift back into neutral" for a "humdrum purpose." This seems like an innocent amusement on Nabokov's part or, since he is the ostensible narrator, a combination of good-humored self-depreciation and bad-humored impatience with people who don't remember his name on Humbert's part. But these prismatically changing colors conceal a literary allusion. The main male character in Joyce's *Finnegans Wake* is Humphrey Chimpden Earwicker. Humphrey's name is subject to a vast variety of mutations, some of which exactly correspond to those of Humbert. For example we find:

Humber, Humhum, Hubbub, Humme, humble Humphrey, Humpty Dumpty, St. Hubert, the hunchback Humphrey, Himmyshimmy, Haromphreyld, Humber was a glommen.

This alone shows Nabokov learned something from Joyce, but there are further allusions.[10] Joyce's main female character (and symbol) is Anna Livia Plurabelle, Humphrey's beloved; Humbert Humbert's early seaside love, responsible for his nymphetmania, is Annabel Leigh (later transmuted into Lolita).[11] Joyce's Humphrey and Anna Plurabelle are symbolic, among other things, of Adam and Eve.[12] Nabokov's Humbert and Annabel play their variations on this Biblical theme. After Annabel, "Humbert was perfectly capable of intercourse with Eve, but it was Lilith [i.e., Lolita, C.P.] he longed for" (p. 22). In his fantasies about possessing Lolita Humbert is "as helpless as Adam . . . in his apple orchard" (p. 73), and when Lolita (alias Annabel, Annabel Lee, Anna Livia Plurabelle, Eve, and Lilith) walks into the Haze living room—for the first time she will be the palpable and unknowing instrument of Humbert's orgasm—she is "holding in her hollowed hands a beautiful, banal, Eden-red apple" (pp. 59–60). As a poet has said, paradise is not paradise without the forbidden fruit. She throws the apple into the air; Humbert intercepts it, but he returns it to her, and as she bites into the apple with sharp desire, he begins his furtive self-manipulation. He says she is "apple-sweet," and he lovingly watches her "devouring her immemorial fruit, singing through its juice" (p. 61). The Adam-Eve-apple theme is continued when Lo wears a gingham dress "with a pattern of little red apples" (p. 113) the day Humbert takes her away from Camp Q. and gorges her with the dearest morsel of the earth.

There are other allusions to Joyce. The name Quilty appears in *Finnegans Wake;* Clare Quilty is Lolita's lover and abductor. The name MacCool also appears in *Finnegans Wake*—suggesting the MacCoo in *Lolita*. Humbert parodies Joyce's *Portrait of the Artist as a Young Man* when, referring to himself, he speaks of seeking a "portrait of an artist as a younger brute." When children in a play wear varicolored veils to represent a rainbow, Humbert comments:

"I remember thinking that this idea of children-colors had been lifted by authors Clare Quilty and Vivian Darkbloom from a passage in Joyce . . ." (p. 223). I haven't located the passage referred to, although "Darkbloom" seems to suggest the Bloom of *Ulysses,* where, in the nighttown section, I find this exchange:

A VOICE
Bloom, are you the Messiah ben Joseph or ben David?
BLOOM
(*Darkly.*) You have said it.[13]

But it appears that this is a spectacular coincidence because "Vivian Darkbloom" is an anagram of "Vladimir Nabokov."

4

After losing Lolita to the playwright Quilty, Humbert begins the mad, futile "cryptogrammic paper chase" from motel to motel[14] in search of clues to her abductor's identity.[15] The shadowy fiend has mocked and mimed Humbert in the signatures he used in motel registers:

His allusions were definitely highbrow. He was well-read. He knew French. He was versed in logodaedaly and logomancy. He was an amateur of sex lore. [pp. 251–52]

Quilty-Nabokov challenges the scholarship of the reader as well as that of Humbert. But fortunately, Humbert often helps his reader decode the literary messages. This section of the novel (Part II, Chapter 23) requires a key. I will simply list the signatures Humbert mentions and provide a brief explanation of each one:

N. Petit, Larousse, Ill.

Pierre Larousse is the famous French lexicographer; his "small" dictionary is well known. "N." is an abbreviation of Nouveau; "Ill." is Illustré as well as Illinois.

At the very first motel office I visited, Ponderosa Lodge, his entry, among a dozen obviously human ones, read: Dr. Gratiano Forbeson, Mirandola, N.Y. Its Italian Comedy connotations could not fail to strike me, of course.

Quilty probably chose the Italian name as appropriate to the "Ponderosa" ("heavy" in Italian) Lodge. I don't know what the heteronational Gratiano Forbeson combination alludes to, but Mirandola must stand for the charming Mirandolina, heroine of Carlo Goldoni's comedy *Mine Hostess.* "Mirandola" means "looking at her"—perhaps Quilty is telling Humbert he is admiring Lo. The letters in the name suggest an anagrammatic relation to Nabokov's name.

"Arsène Lupin" was obvious to a Frenchman who remembered the detective stories of his youth.

Maurice Leblanc was the author of a number of detective novels in which Lupin is the sleuthing protagonist.

---

one hardly had to be a Coleridgian to appreciate the trite poke of "A. Person, Porlock, England."

Coleridge reported that when he was writing down his dream-vision of the lines of *Kubla Khan,* he was interrupted "by a person on business from Porlock and detained by him above one hour"—after which he could not recollect the details of his vision and ceased writing.[16]

"Arthur Rainbow"—plainly travestied the author of *Le Bateau Bleu*—let me laugh a little, too, gentlemen—and "Morris Schmetterling," of *L'Oiseau Ivre* fame. (touché, reader!)

Among the works of Arthur Rimbaud is *Le Bateau Ivre.* One of Maurice Maeterlinck's best-known plays is *L'Oiseau Bleu.* Quilty travesties the names; Humbert reverses the adjectives *bleu* and *ivre* for his own laugh. Later in the murder scene Quilty says: "I have been called the American Maeterlinck. Maeterlinck-Schmetterling, says I." *Schmetterling* is the German for "butterfly," which fits in nicely with the "rainbow" and "bird" as well as with Nabokov's passionate avocation.

The silly but funny "D. Orgon, Elmira, N.Y." was from Molière, of course . . .

In Molière's *Tartuffe,* Orgon and his wife Elmire are under the hypocrite's power. "D. Orgon" is a *double-entendre:* the organ. Since Nabokov is a violent anti-Freudian, this might also refer to Wilhelm Reich's weird theories about orgasms and orgone.[17]

. . . because I had quite recently tried to interest Lolita in a famous 18th-century play, I welcomed as an old friend "Harry Bumper, Sheridan, Wyo."

Another phallic intrusion: "a hairy bumper" or "Harry, bump her." Harry Bumper is a minor character in Richard Sheridan's *A School for Scandal*. He sings a song beginning: "Here's to the maid of bashful fifteen," and containing the line: "And here's to the nymph . . ." (Act III, Scene 3).

An ordinary encyclopedia informed me who the peculiar look-ing "Phineas Quimby, Lebanon, N.H." was . . .

It is as Humbert promises. According to *Britannica,* Phineas P. Quimby (1802–60), born in Lebanon, N.H., was a hypno-tist. "His experiments extended through mental suggestion to mental healing, sometimes accompanied by physical manipulation." The encyclopedia's comment, inadvertently, I am sure, sounds obscene—which would amuse Humbert and fit: Quim = vagina, Quimby = Quilty.

. . . and any good Freudian, with a German name and some interest in religious prostitution, should recognize at a glance the implications of "Dr. Kitzler, Eryx, Miss."

Kitzler is the German for "clitoris," *ergo,* Dr. Clitoris. On Mt. Eryx in Sicily there was a temple to Venus. The priestesses were prostitutes, i.e. Eryx Misses. The Mount of Venus also comes to mind.

In addition this suggests references made earlier in the novel. Near Lolita's camp (Camp Q. = Camp Quilty? or

Camp Quim?) are three lakes: Lake Climax and Lakes
Onyx and Eryx. In one of Humbert's sexual fantasies he
sees a slave girl climbing "a column of onyx"—which any
good Freudian should recognize as a smooth phallic symbol
(p. 136).

Then Humbert writes:

Among entries that arrested my attention as undoubtable
clues *per se* but baffled me in respect to their finer points I do
not care to mention many since I feel I am groping in a border-
land mist with verbal phantoms turning, perhaps, into living
vacationists. Who was "Johnny Randall, Ramble, Ohio"? Or
was he a real person who just happened to write a hand similar
to "N. S. Aristoff, Catagela, N.Y." What was the sting in "Catagela"? And what about James Mavor Morell, Hoaxton, England"? "Aristophanes," "hoax,"—fine, but what was I missing?
[pp. 252–53]

The "Johnny Randall" allusion is a hard one—perhaps it
refers to Sam Johnson's *The Rambler* (1749–52), a journal
of literature and essays (mostly Johnson's own). The bawdy
ballad "Lord Randall" is an appropriate possibility. Or it
could be an allusion to Cecilia Dalrymple Ramble, who
donated a bench to Beardsley College (p. 254). Catagela is
the punningly comic name of a nonexistent city in Aristophanes' *Archarnians* (l. 606). The name is derived from the
Greek verb *katagelao*, "to sneer," "to smirk." This is the
"sting" Humbert does not feel. James Mavor Morell is one
of the characters in George Bernard Shaw's *Candida,* and
Hoxton is one of the towns where the play is set.[18]
    The orgy of allusions continues:

"G. Trapp, Geneva, N.Y." was a sign of treachery on Lolita's part. [p. 253]

Gustave Trapp was Humbert's Swiss uncle; Humbert told Lolita the man trailing them resembled Trapp.

———

"Aubrey Beardsley, Quelquepart Island" suggested . . . the starting point of the affair should be looked for in the East. [p. 253]

Aubrey Beardsley (1872–98) was the decadent art editor of the *Yellow Book* and *The Savoy,* illustrator of a number of works, including Oscar Wilde's *Salome.* Beardsley is the name of the town (and the school) where Lolita takes her mystery lover. Aubrey McFate, according to the class-list of Ramsdale School, was one of Lo's classmates. (And Humbert often refers to fate as McFate after reading the list.) *Quel*quepar*t I*sland = Quilty. And there is a Quelpart Island in Canada.

———

"Lucas Picador, Merrymay, Pa." insinuated my Carmen had betrayed my pathetic endearments to the imposter. [p. 253]

Humbert often calls Lolita Carmen. In Prosper Merimée's story *Carmen,* the heroine leaves her lover for a picador named Lucas (Lucas = Quilty).[19]

———

Horribly cruel, forsooth, was "Will Brown, Dolores, Colo." [p. 253]

In the preceding chapter (22), Humbert composes this poem:

> *Saint,* forsooth! While brown Dolores,
> On a patch of sunny green
> With Sanchicha reading stories
> In a movie magazine—[p. 247]

This is odd, because Quilty had no knowledge of these verses—so he couldn't have chosen "Will Brown" to mock Humbert's "While brown." On the other hand brown is the color most often associated with Lolita (and Annabel), and Quilty would know that. (One should also keep in mind the fact that Humbert is quite mad and may be hallucinating all this.) But more important is the fact that Quilty knew the poem Humbert had parodied in composing his verses— Robert Browning's "Soliloquy of the Spanish Cloister," the fourth stanza of which begins:

> Saint, forsooth! While brown Dolores
> Squats outside the Convent bank
> With Sanchicha, telling stories
> Steeping tresses in the tank . . .

———————

The gruesome "Harold Haze, Tombstone, Arizona" . . . implied a familiarity with the girl's past that in nightmare fashion suggested for a moment that my quarry [i.e. Quilty, C.P.] was an old friend of the family, maybe an old flame of Charlotte's, maybe a redresser of wrongs ("Donald Quix, Sierra, Nev."). [p. 253]

Harold Haze, the original HH, was Lolita's father; he had died a few years before. The Sierra Nevada redresser of wrongs is Don Quixote. Also *Quix* = *Quilty.*

———————

But the most penetrating bodkin of all was the anagram-tailed entry in the register of Chestnut Lodge: "Ted Hunter, Cane, N.H." [p. 253]

The anagram-tail is from The Enchan*ted Hunters*, the hotel whose name appears in various forms all through the novel. This is the most penetrating bodkin because (apart from suggesting Humbert's successful rival knew all about The Enchanted Hunters) it tells us that Quilty had stayed at the Chestnut Lodge at the same time Humbert and Lolita did. Or rather, it will tell us if we remember some other details and make the connections. Earlier Humbert notes: "Only in one case had he actually stayed at the same motor court as we, a few paces from Lolita's pillow" (p. 250). If we follow this clue back to the Chestnut Lodge pages, we discover that Lolita had been making love to Quilty while Humbert Humbert was in Kasbeam getting a "very mediocre haircut" (p. 215). This can be deduced from two things. When Humbert returns to the lodge he finds her "dreamily brimmed with a diabolical glow that had no relation to me whatever" (p. 216). And in his description of the motel Humbert notes only a few cars, but from one garage "a red hood protruded in somewhat cod-piece fashion" (p. 215). The "red hood," we can conclude, belongs to the infamous Aztec Red Convertible which will appear during the next days and make Humbert grow grim about the mouth. Quilty is following Lolita. The phallic protrusion of the red "cod-piece" makes it a "penetrating bodkin" indeed.

There are also literary allusions in the few license numbers which Humbert remembers. He says:

The license of the initial Aztec was a shimmer of shifting numerals, some transposed, others altered or omitted, but somehow forming interrelated combinations (such as "WS1564" and "SH1616," and "Q32888" or "CU88322") which however were so cunningly contrived as to never reveal a common denominator. [p. 253]

The first two stand for William Shakespeare, born 1564, Shakespeare died 1616. The cunningly contrived common denominator of the second pair eludes me. "Q" and "CU" obviously stand for "Quilty" and "Cue." And I suspect that somehow (perhaps all of the eights are fours doubled) 342 must be the basis for the two numbers.[20]

5

Chapter 23 of Part II contains more allusions than any other chapter, but literary associations run through the whole novel. In the great majority of cases the allusions are not "contextual," by which I mean that the context of the work quoted (or misquoted, or parodied) has no direct relevance for characters or situations in *Lolita*. These allusions are rather like old acquaintances who suddenly appear on a street: we may wave and say hello to them, but we need not pause to inquire into their inner life. For example, Quilty addresses Humbert "Now look here, Mac" and then puns:

"I have not much at the bank right now, but I propose to borrow—you know, as the Bard said, with that cold in his head, to borrow and to borrow and to borrow." [p. 303]

The content of the "tomorrow and tomorrow and tomorrow" speech in *MacBeth* (V, 5, 19) which he parodies has no relevance for this scene in *Lolita*.[21] The same is true of the following three-limbed alliterative allusion. Humbert sits beside Lo at a soda fountain:

You have a lovely child, Mr. Humbert. We always admire her as she passes by. Mr. Pim watched Pippa suck in the concoction.
J'ai toujours admiré l'oeuvre ormonde du sublime Dublinois.
[p. 209]

Pippa is the poor, sweet, sewing-girl heroine of Robert Browning's dramatic poem *Pippa Passes*.[22] As "Pippa passes by"—the phrase is repeated several times in the poem—her holiday songs affect the lives of the people who hear them, a fact of which she is unaware. *Mr. Pim* is the title and hero of an obscure novel by A. A. Milne.[23] The ultramundane *(ormonde)* work of the sublime Dubliner is Joyce's *Ulysses,* where:

Above the crossblind of the Ormond Hotel, gold by bronze, Miss Kennedy's head by Miss Douce's head watched and admired. On Ormond quay Mr. Simon Dedalus . . . Bronze by gold, Miss Douce's head by Miss Kennedy's head, over the crossblind of the Ormond bar heard the viceregal hoofs go by, ringing steel.[24]

It is curious that there are so few allusions to Russian literature; I suppose Nabokov got most of these out of his system in earlier works, especially *The Gift*. But a few do remain. Chekhov and Dostoevsky are referred to by name. The phrase "everything was allowed" (p. 270) used by Humbert (regarding immoral acts) suggests *The Brothers Karamazov*.[25] When Humbert revisits Ramsdale, he notes: "As in a Turgenev story, a torrent of Italian music came from an open window—that of the living room . . ." (p. 290). Turgenev has a weakness for this kind of thing in general; his *Spring Waters* is one specific example. I have sometimes thought Charlotte's letter of confession to Humbert was a wild travesty of Tatyana's letter to Eugene Onegin; that

would probably be stretching a point, but there is an allusion to Pushkin's *The Gypsies*. This may be nonsense, but
Charlotte's twice-repeated and prim *"Ne montrez pas vos
zhambes" (sic)*, suggests a notorious monostich by the
Russian decadent poet Valery Bryusov: "O, cover thy pale
legs." The end of Chapter 10 (Part II) is an allusion to
Gogol. Humbert says, "But never mind, never mind, I am
only a brute, never mind, let us go on with my miserable
story" (p. 195). In Gogol's *Notes of a Madman* (which would
be a good alternate title for *Lolita*) the first-person diarist
Poprishchin keeps repeating: *nichevo, nichevo, molchanie—*
"never mind, never mind, silence."

The great majority of allusions, however, are to French
and English literature. For one thing, this fits Humbert's
background and tastes. The list I have compiled follows,
but it is by no means complete. There are many phrases and
sentences which I am sure are allusions, but I have been
unable to idenitfy them. And there must be many I do not
even recognize as being allusions. Arranged alphabetically
for the sake of convenience, here is the list of those which
are not, to use a Balzacian phrase, lost allusions. (Many of
the names are mentioned directly in *Lolita;* those which
aren't are either footnoted here or explained elsewhere in
my text.)

> Alcott, Louisa May
> Andersen, Hans Christian[26]
> Aristophanes
> Baudelaire, Charles
> Belleau, Remy[27]
> Belloc, Hilaire
> Blake, William
> Browning, Robert

Bürger, August[28]
Carroll, Lewis
Catullus
Cervantes, Miguel
Chateaubriand, François René
Chekhov, Anton Pavlovich
Christie, Agatha
Cocteau, Jean
Coleridge, Samuel Taylor
Cowper, William
Dante
Dostoevsky, F. M.
Doyle, Arthur Conan
Flaubert, Gustave[29]
Galsworthy, John
Gide, André
Goethe, Wolfgang
Gogol, Nikolai Vasilievich
Goldoni, Carlo
Hopkins, Gerard Manley
Hugo, Victor
Ibsen, Henrik
Joyce, James[30]
Keats, John[31]
Kilmer, Joyce
Kipling, Rudyard[32]
Lenormand, Henri-René
Maeterlinck, Maurice
Marlowe, Christopher
Maturin, Charles Robert
Melville, Herman[33]
Milne, A. A.
Ovid

Petrarch
Poe, Edgar A.
Poquelin, Jean-Baptiste
Proust, Marcel
Pushkin, Alexander
Rimbaud, Arthur
Rolland, Romain
Ronsard, Pierre de[34]
Rostand, Edmond
Rousseau, Jean-Jacques
Sade, Donatien-Alphonse-
    François, comte de
Scott, Walter[35]
Shakespeare, William
Shaw, George Bernard
Sheridan, Richard
Sophocles
Stevenson, Robert Louis
Stowe, Harriet Beecher
Swinburne, Algernon Charles
Turgenev, Ivan Sergeevich
Verlaine, Paul
Virgil

There are non-literary allusions, too.[36] For example, when Humbert lives with Valeria in Paris they have a flat:

. . . two rooms, a *hazy* view in one window, a brick wall in the other, a tiny kitchen, a shoe-shaped bath tub, within which I felt like Marat but with no white-necked maiden to stab me. [p. 28, C.P.'s italics]

If his mind's eye could have penetrated the "hazy view," Humbert would have known that one day he would have

his own Charlotte—Haze rather than Corday. Another reference to French history occurs when he gleefully imagines
entering Camp Q disguised as a woman; he hopes the russet
nymphs will find "her" and ". . . drag the sad, shyly smiling
Berthe *au Grand Pied* to their rustic hearth. Berthe will
sleep with Dolores Haze" (p. 68). Berthe was Charlemagne's
slightly asymmetrical mother. There is a *chanson de geste*
about her by the thirteenth-century minstrel Adenet le
Roi.[37] Berthe (daughter of Blanchefleur) has several misad-
ventures on her way to be wed, and the work ends rather
abruptly as she sets off alone into the deep dark forest—
from which, in the guise of Humbert, she emerges a millen-
nium or so later.

    History and literary myth also merge in the archaic names
of the Farlows' dogs, Cavall and Melampus. Cavall was
King Arthur's dog. Melampus was a seer whose ears,
according to Greek mythology, had been cleansed by the
tongues of serpents so that he could comprehend the
speech of animals. The philistine Farlows aren't imaginative enough to find such names for their dogs, but Nabokov is.[38]

    I have said that most of the literary allusions are not
contextual. However, there are a number of allusions in
which it is essential to know the original context of the quotation, name, or theme used. For example, at the beginning
of Chapter 14, Part II, Humbert informs us that he allowed
Lo to take bi-weekly piano lessons "with a Miss Emperor
(as we French scholars may conveniently call her)," but
that near the end of May:

. . . the telephone in my study, where I was in the act of mop-
ping up Gustave's—I mean Gaston's—king's side, rang and Miss

Emperor asked if Lo was coming next Tuesday, because she had missed last Tuesday's and today's lessons.

A little later Humbert interrogates Lolita:

She remained singularly unruffled when confronted with my discovery, and said *d'un petit air faussement contrit* that she knew she was a very wicked kid, but had simply not been able to resist the enchantment. . . .

and that she had spent those hours rehearsing "the magic forest scene with Mona," referring to the play then being prepared by the Beardsley girls. —It will turn out (the chain of clues is discussed in detail in the next chapter) that she was with her new lover, Clare Quilty, instead of with Miss Emperor. This entire episode parallels one in the life of Gustave Flaubert's Madame Bovary (Part III, Chapter 5). Instead of taking Thursday pianoforte lessons as she tells her husband, Emma is tying the lover's knot with Léon (in *un grand lit d'acajou en forme de nacelle*). Things are going as easily as a knife through butter and:

Emma was living without any apprehensions when one evening abruptly:
   "It's Mlle. Lempereur who is giving you lessons, isn't it?"
   "Yes."
   "Well, I saw her just now at Mme. Liégeard's" Charles went on. "I spoke to her about you: she doesn't know you."
   It was like a thunderclap. She answered, however, in a natural manner:
   "Oh, I suppose she must have forgotten my name."[39]

Charles supposes that there are several Mlles. Lempereur teaching piano in Rouen. Emma supposes there are, too. Then she says she has receipts, but can't find them; and it is not until the next Friday that Charles discovers, in his shoe, this document:

Received for three months lessons plus various supplies, the sum of sixty-five francs.

F E L I C I E L'E M P E R E U R
Professeur de musique

Forged, of course. Even if the reader does not recognize the Emma-parallel in *Lolita,* other indications will enable him to interpret this episode, to conclude what lesson Lo was getting, and who her lover was—but he misses the pleasure deriving from the literary association, the awareness that one is hearing a variation on a theme.

Are there other instances where it is essential to remember the original context in which a quotation or name appears? Yes. —Take the case of Lolita's literary antecedents, the fictional forebears to whom Humbert so often alludes. They may be divided into two groups, the demonic and the angelic: "De Satan ou de Dieu, qu'importe? Ange ou Sirène?" Both sides (Humbert himself notes) are joined in every nymphet. On the heavenly side are Beatrice, Laureen, Annabel Lee, Pippa, and perhaps Juliet. On the hellish side are Lilith, Rahab, the Vampire, Zemfira, Carmen, and Dolores. Lilith (wife of Adam and/or consort of the devil) has already been mentioned; Annabel is discussed in Section Six below; Zemfira and Carmen in Section Seven. Let's look at the others now.

Attempting to justify his tastes by citing historical precedents, mad Humbert distorts a few of the facts and adds some details. For example, he asserts:

After all, Dante fell madly in love with his Beatrice when

she was nine, a sparkling girleen, painted and lovely, and
bejewelled, in a crimson frock, and this was in 1274, in Flor-
ence, at a private feast in the merry month of May. And when
Petrarch fell madly in love with his Laureen, she was a fair-
haired nymphet of twelve running in the wind, in the pollen
and dust, a flower in flight, in the beautiful plain as descried
from the hills of Vaucluse. [p. 121]

Dante's first meeting with Beatrice is described in his *Vita
Nuova;* he doesn't specify the month. Petrarch didn't fall
in love with Laureen (*Laura–Lolita?*) when she was twelve
and running through the pollen near Vaucluse. She was
about eighteen, and it was in the church of St. Clara in
Avignon (April 6, 1327). —Incidentally, she was wearing
green and bedecked in violets. It is true that many of the
poems about her were written in Vaucluse.

The female demons are rather more numerous than the
female angels, and, as is usually the case, more interesting.
Rahab for example: "Hugh Broughton, a writer of contro-
versy in the reign of James the First, has proved that Rahab
was a harlot at ten years of age" (p. 21). Broughton (1549–
1612) did exist and did write on the Bible, though I haven't
researched Humbert's other information. Rahab was the
Biblical harlot of Jericho. (Originally Rahab was the name
of an evil spirit animating the primeval ocean.) In William
Blake's *The Four Zoas*, Rahab is a Satanic female, "A False
Feminine Counterpart, of Lovely Delusive Beauty, Divid-
ing and Uniting at Will in the Cruelties of Holiness"; she
seeks dominion by using sex. This certainly fits Humbert's
Lolita. Humbert notes that one night he picked up R*ita*
(Lol*ita*'s substitute) "between Toylestown and Blake, at a
darkishly burning bar under the sign of the Tigermoth"

(p. 260). This suggests Blake's famous "Tyger" burning bright in the forests of the night.

A more difficult allusion is the following:

. . . a *brun adolescent* whom her russet beauty and the quick-silver in the baby folds of her stomach were sure to cause to *se tordre*—oh Baudelaire!—[p. 164]

Unquestionably, the poem Humbert has in mind is *Les Metamorphoses du Vampire.* The first two stanzas are especially appropriate:

> La femme cependant, de sa bouche de fraise,
> En *se tordant* ainsi qu'un serpent sur la braise,
> Et pétrissant ses seins sur le fer de son busc,
> Laissait couler ces mots tout imprégnés de musc:
> —"Moi, j'ai la lèvre humide, et ja sais la science
> De perde au fond d'un lit l'antique conscience.
> Je sèche tous les pleurs sur mes seins triomphants,
> Et fais rire les vieux du rire des enfants.
> Je remplace, pour qui me voit nue et sans voiles,
> La lune, le soleil, le ciel et les étoiles!
> Je suis, mon cher savant, si docte aux voluptés,
> Lorsque j'étouffe un homme en mes bras redoutés,
> Ou lorsque j'abandonne aux morsures mon buste,
> Timide et libertine, et fragile et robuste,
> Que sur ces matelas qui se pâment d'émoi,
> Les anges impuissants se damneraient pour moi!"[40]

It is clear that Humbert sees certain parallels.

Lo has some actual namesakes among the demonic ladies of literature too. The most important literary echo of her real name, Dolores Haze, is from Algernon Swinburne's "Dolores"—subtitled *Notre-Dame des Sept Douleurs:* thereby paralleling Humbert's various puns on Dolores (dolorous darling, dumps and dolors, *adolori*, etc.).[41] Dolores is "Our Lady of Pain," and among the pertinent lines are these:

> Wert thou pure and a maiden, Dolores,
>   When desire took thee first by the throat?
> What bud was the shell of a blossom
>   That all men may smell to and pluck?
>
> No thorne's go as deep as a rose's.[42]
>   And love is more cruel than lust.
>
> Fierce midnights and famishing morrows,
>   And the loves that complete and control
> All the joys of the flesh, all the sorrows
>   That wear out the soul.

And especially:

> There are sins it may be to discover,
>   There are deeds it may be to delight.
> What new work wilt thou find for thy lover
>   What new passions for daytime or night?
> What spells that they know not a word of
>   Whose lives are as leaves overblown?
> What tortures undreamt of, unheard of,
>   Unwritten, unknown?

Humbert says if all girl children were nymphic ("That is, demoniac"), "we who are in the know, we lone voyagers, we nympholepts, would have long ago gone insane" (pp. 18–19) because they possess an "elusive, shifty, soul-shattering, insidious charm." After Annabel, "the poison was in the wound," and in jail he summarizes:

I am trying to describe these things not to relive them in my present boundless misery, but to sort out the portion of hell and the portion of heaven in that strange awful maddening world—nymphet love. [p. 137]

He says his elected world is a "paradise whose skies were the color of hell-flame" (p. 168).[43] He is the first to discover these sins and record them, these torments and spells unwritten, unheard of, unknown before Humbert Humbert composes his memoir. Apparently it amuses Nabokov's genius to rely on reverberations from third-rate works like "Dolores."[44]

When we proceed from his heroine's legal name to her Humbertish name, we find another example of this whimsy. The only literary Lolita[45] I have been able to find who antedates our girl is in a play by Lenormand, *La Maison des Remparts*. (Humbert alludes to Lenormand later—see below, p. 145.) Lenormand's Lolita is a *belle brune*, twenty-one years old, slightly—and poetically—mad (like two of Chekhov's sisters she imagines being a bird). Following the death of her parents (like our Lo, she did not love her mother), she is taken away from her Central American home by a Frenchman who is ultimately responsible for debauching her—she is twelve years old at the time—and putting her in a French bordello. The nymphet's demon-angel nature is made clear by speeches like: *"Je voudrais parler avec la Vierge et les saints. Des fois, aussi, avec le diable."* She believes, *"Les hommes sont absurdes,"* and her lament at the end of the play echoes things Humbert's Lolita might well think (though never say).

Pense donc! Chaque partie de son corps,—chaque centimètre de sa peau,—touché, écrasé, frotté, sali, par des mains, par des ventres, par des cuisses, par des lèvres d'ivrognes! Et son trésor, violé, lavé, reviolé, relavé, désinfecté, inspecté! . . . Oh! André! André! (Elle éclate en sanglots.) Et sa bouche, qu'elle est faite pour chanter, ou pour dire des mots d'amour . . . sa bouche, elle essuie le déssir des broutes, des insensés, des vieillards, des malades![46]

Of course, in some ways Humbert is a sick brute, madman and (for Lo) a *vieillard*. The similarities are sufficient to make me think it is likely that Lenormand's whore belongs in the twin constellation of beauties shining over the shoulder of Lolita Haze.

A list of allusions in which knowledge of the original context is essential must include the name Humbert the Hound gives to his car: Melmoth. If we know the title of Charles Robert Maturin's once-popular Gothic novel—*Melmoth the Wanderer*—we recognize the allusion, but some knowledge of the sinister deeds of the nefarious eternal wanderer is essential if we are to see how appropriate (or inappropriate) a name the monster-poet Humbert has chosen for his vehicle (a distant descendant of Chichikov's carriage).[47] Another allusion where the context of the source is important is used when Hum and Lolita are being pursued by the mystery car. Humbert notes:

We were many times weaker than his splendid, lacquered machine, so that I did not even attempt to outspeed him. *O lente currite noctis equi!* O softly run, nightmares! [p. 221]

Humbert puns *noctis equi* (lit. "horses of the night"—in the mythological sense) into nightmares, borrowing a line which has double associations. In Christopher Marlowe's *The Tragicall History of Doctor Faustus* the clock strikes eleven,

and Faustus has but one hour to live before perpetual dam-
nation. He implores the "moving spheres of heaven" to
stand still that he may repent and save his soul:

> *O lente, lente currite noctis equi:*
> The starres moove stil, time runs, the clock wil strike,
> The diuel wil come, and Faustus must be damnd.
>
> [ll. 1428–30]

Certainly Humbert Humbert sees his fiendish pursuer as a
devil, and the time when he will be damned (by losing Lo)
is not far away. Why does that which makes a man happy
have to become the source of his misery?

Even more appropriate than *Faustus* is the context of the
Latin line in its original source, Ovid's *Loves*, I, XIII, 40.
The poet beseeches Aurora not to come, for the day brings
many bad consequences, the most important being that
not-yet-exhausted lovers have to part. Aurora is fleeing from
her husband "because he is old":

> But if you held in your arms the form of the mortal you
> wanted,
> Then you would cry, "Run slowly, slowly, horses of
> the night!"
> Is it my fault as a lover, if yours is old and disgusting?
> Is it my fault you married this tiresome old man?[48]

With a slight twist of irony, the applicability of this for
the tiresome, disgusting Humbert Humbert and his lover
Lolita is clear.

Later in the chronicle, Humbert describes his second visit
to Briceland (home of The Enchanted Hunters) with Rita:

A curious urge to relive my stay there with Lolita had got hold
of me. . . . I now attempted to fall back on old settings in order

to save what could still be saved in the way of *souvenir, souvenir, que me veux-tu?* Autumn was ringing in the air. [p. 263]

Among Verlaine's *Poëmes Saturiens* are two lyrics entitled (in English) "Nevermore." One begins:

> Souvenir, souvenir, que me veux-tu? L'automne
> Faisait voler la grive à travers l'air atone. . . .

The poet and his lover are walking alone when suddenly she asks, "*Quel fut ton plus beau jour?*" He kisses her hand and replies:

> —Ah! les premières fleurs, qu'elles sont parfumées!
> Et qu'il bruit avec un murmure charmant
> Le premier *oui* qui sort de lèvres bien-aimées!

Humbert associates The Enchanted Hunters with Lolita's "first yes," explaining why he recalls Verlaine's poem when he does. The allusion within the allusion is one of the multiple references to Poe (discussed in the next section).[49]

Another example: hanging over the bed in the room Humbert rents from Charlotte Haze is a copy of René Prinet's "Kreutzer Sonata." Beethoven is inapplicable, but in Tolstoy's story *The Kreutzer Sonata*, the sex-mad protagonist murders his wife. We know from the beginning of the novel that Humbert is in prison, that he is probably a murderer. Nabokov-Humbert delights in misleading his readers with false associations, and this is one of them—it soon appears to anyone who knows Tolstoy's story that Humbert will murder his wife, Charlotte. In this case, as in others I will discuss, the well-read reader who tries to anticipate events will be cruelly deceived.

6

Humbert alludes to Edgar Allan Poe's "Annabel Lee" and Prosper Merimée's *Carmen* more often than to any other work or writer.[50] Untwisting this string of allusions is like trying to straighten out the spiral of a DNA molecule; and the complicated way the echoes and quotations are coiled and fitted into the text makes it extremely difficult[51] to separate them and attempt to present them in the form of an essay. Until the whole pattern is seen and comprehended, individual allusions seem to be of little consequence. If the reader will bear this in mind, I will begin with Annabel Lee. For Humbert declares:

I am convinced, however, that in a certain magic and fateful way Lolita began with Annabel. [pp. 15–16]

Given Nabokov's subtle ear for sound, I don't think it is hyperinterpretation to note the reversal of the initial and terminal letters in the two names Annabel-Lolita. Lolita is a reincarnation of Annabel Leigh. As Humbert remarks when he sees Lo for the first time: "There was my Riviera love peering at me over dark glasses" (p. 41). He feels like a king who has discovered a lost princess—from a princedom by the sea. Here are some pertinent lines from Poe's poem:

> It was many and many a year ago
>   In a kingdom by the sea,
> That a maiden there lived whom you may know
>   By the name of ANNABEL LEE; . . .
> I was a child and she was a child,
>   In this kingdom by the sea;
> But we loved with a love that was more than love—

> I and my ANNABEL LEE;
> With a love that the winged seraphs of heaven
>   Coveted her and me.
> The angels, not half so happy in heaven,
>   Went envying her and me . . .

A chill angel-sent wind takes her life, but, says the poet, neither angel nor demon:

> Can ever dissever my soul from the soul
>   Of the beautiful ANNABEL LEE . . .
> And so, all the night-tide, I lie down by the side
> *Of my darling—my darling—my life and my bride*[52]
>   In the sepulchre there by the sea,
>   In her tomb by the sounding sea.

Chapter 1, the brilliant lyrical overture to *Lolita*, is pervaded with suggestions of this poem:

> Lolita, *light of my life*, fire of my loins. My sin *my soul* . . .
> . . . there might have been no Lolita at all *had I not loved*, one summer, a certain initial *girl-child. In a princedom by the sea.* Oh when? About as *many years* before Lolita was born as my age was that summer. . . .
>   Ladies and gentlemen of the jury, exhibit number one *is what the seraphs,* the misinformed, simple, *noble-winged seraphs, envied.*

Throughout the novel Humbert calls Lolita "my darling" or "my darling—oh my darling" with a regularity which suggests it is not just the conventional term of affection. The literary umbilicals connecting Poe's Annabel Lee, Humbert's Riviera Annabel Leigh, and Lolita are quite apparent:

> My darling . . . smelt almost exactly like the other one, the Riviera one, only more intensely so . . . [p. 44]

When I was a child and she was a child, my little Annabel was no nymphet to me . . . [p. 19]

I shall probably have another breakdown if I stay any longer in this house, under the strain of this intolerable temptation, *by the side of my darling—my darling—my life and my bride.* [p. 49]

Other echoes of Poe resound in Humbert's apostrophes to the jury above:

Winged gentlemen! [p. 232]

Oh, winged gentlemen of the jury! And she was mine, she was mine . . . [p. 127]

The winged gentlemen are Poe's "winged seraphs of heaven"; the anapestic lilt and accented "i's" (as in "light of my life," "my life and my bride") of "she was mine" are further reflections and reverberations of Poe. Elsewhere Humbert-Nabokov even imitates Poe's syntax:

. . . we would become strangely embarrassed whenever I tried to discuss something she and an older friend, she and a parent, she and a real healthy sweetheart, *I and Annabel,* Lolita . . . and Harold Haze might have discussed. [p. 286]

The inversion "I and Annabel" seems to follow from the other inversions in the sentence; actually it follows a century-old poem:

But we loved with a love that was more than love—
I and my ANNABEL LEE . . .

I suspect another Lolita-related inversion is a muffled echo of Poe's tombal music:

In the velvet night, at Mirana Motel (Mirana!)[53]
I kissed the yellowish soles of her long-toed feet . . .
Both doomed were we. [p. 229]

One more reminder of "Annabel Lee":

A little later, of course, she this *nouvelle,* this Lolita, *my* Lolita, was to eclipse completely her prototype. All I want to stress is that my discovery of her was a fatal consequence of that "princedom by the sea" in my tortured past . . . [pp. 41–42, italics in original]

One of the reasons why it is entirely apposite for Humbert to employ citations from "Annabel Lee" relates to the biography of the poem's author: Poe married his cousin Virginia Clem when she was only thirteen years old. Humbert sees a parallel: "Oh Lolita, you are my girl, as Vee was Poe's and Bea Dante's . . ." (p. 109). He often uses historical, anthropological, and literary data to justify his taste for youth,[54] thus he records that:

Virginia was not quite fourteen when Harry Edgar possessed her.[55] He gave her lessons in algebra. *Je m'imagine cela.* They spent their honeymoon at Petersburg, Fla.[56] "Monsieur Poepoe," as that boy in one of Monsieur Humbert Humbert's classes in Paris called the poet-poet. [p. 45]

Soon Charlotte asks Humbert to help Lo with her homework in geography, mathematics, and French. And the Poe allusions continue when in the interview for the Ramsdale paper Humbert gives his name as "Mr. Edgar H. Humbert," ("I threw in the 'Edgar' just for the heck of it").[57] He again borrows Poe's Christian name when he signs the register at The Enchanted Hunters "Dr. Edgar H. Humbert." He uses the same name later in Beardsley.

Finally, Edgar Allan Humbert-Poe alludes to "The Raven" and the closely related "Lenore" when he says to Lolita:

"Now hop-hop-hop, Lenore, or you'll get soaked." (A storm of sobs was filling my chest.)

She bared her teeth and after her adorable school-girl fashion, leaned forward, and *away she sped, my bird.* [p. 209][58]

To refresh the reader's memory, and as a last piece of "raw material" before suggesting some reasons for the use of these allusions, I will quote some pertinent lines from "The Raven":

> Oh, distinctly I remember it was in the bleak December,[59]
> . . . .
> . . . vainly I had sought to borrow
> From my books surcease of sorrow—sorrow for the lost
>   Lenore. . . .
> "Wretch," I cried, "thy God hath lent thee—by these
>   angels he hath sent thee
> Respite—respite and nepenthe from thy memories of
>   Lenore!
> Quaff, oh quaff this kind nepenthe and forget this lost
>   Lenore!"
> Quoth the Raven, "Nevermore."

And from "Lenore":[60]

> See on yon drear and rigid bier low lies thy love, Lenore!
> Come! let the burial rite be read—the funeral song be
>   sung!—
> An anthem for the queenliest dead that ever died so young—
> A dirge for her the doubly dead in that she died so young.
>
> The sweet Lenore hath "gone before," with Hope, that
>   flew beside,
> Leaving thee wild for the dear child that should have
>   been thy bride[61]
> To friends above from fiends below, the indignant
>   ghost is riven.[62]

Why all the allusions to Poe and his poetry? Is this just another cryptogrammic paper chase to amuse the writer and his readers? I think not. It is true there is an element of this literary whimsy involved; and a reader derives some pleasure just from his ability to recognize the allusion, particularly the more recherché ones. But the Poe allusions go beyond this diverting and clever but not very profound game of wit and memory.

The common denominator in all three of the Poe poems is the death of a very young woman.[63] In *Lolita* the most important of the three is "Annabel Lee"—which was written not long after the early death of the original Annabel, Poe's child-bride Virginia. If Lolita-Annabel is Humbert's girl "as Vee was Poe's," it seems reasonable for the reader to expect Lolita's death.[64] The death theme in "Lenore" and "The Raven" seems to reinforce this conclusion. Humbert, we know from the very beginning, is in prison for murder; so if we add two and two, it appears we may expect Humbert to murder Lolita.[65] Unfortunately, in Nabokov's prose two and two usually equal three, seven or the square root of minus one—which, of course, is a very nice thing sometimes. What appears to be the murder of Humbert's queen turns out to be Nabokov's ace in the hole. The trail of deception goes something like this: At first we are led, by allusion, to suspect Lolita will be his victim; this may be a very vague feeling initially, but the Carmen allusions lend it great strength. Then when Charlotte Haze enters the picture and must be dealt with, there is a reversal—it seems certain Humbert will murder her, and in the Hourglass Lake scene (Chapter 20) Nabokov leads us up to the very last instant fostering this belief. Humbert uses impeccable logic to carry out (mentally) the perfect crime. Then Humbert smilingly dismisses the possibility of the act we have been led to anticipate.[66]

But what d'ye know, folks—I just could not make myself do it. [p. 89]

In spite of this slap in the face, the reader still has to keep Charlotte in mind as a possible if not a likely candidate for Humbert's hostility. Nabokov parallels a situation in Charles Perrault's *Barbe Bleuë* (1697) to lend apparent substance to our suspicions. Bluebeard's wife is condemned to death only after she uses a mysterious and forbidden key which reveals her husband's secret (a large wardrobe crammed with cadavers). The evil husband—curious wife— little key—box—murderous secret revealed pattern again suggests Humbert will at least try to murder Charlotte— until, of course, we see that her death is an accident for which Humbert is responsible, but not prosecutable.[67] Immediately, the reader must choose another victim for Humbert, and the choice shifts back to Lolita with certainty now—it has been suggested by the "Annabel Lee" and other Poe allusions—and reinforced by the repeated allusions to Carmen (which I will discuss below). The reader who (1) recognizes all the allusions, (2) draws logical parallels, (3) is not cautious, will go through much of the novel anticipating an untimely end for the heroine.

A less tangible function of "Annabel Lee" in *Lolita* is related to style, to an emotional tone which pervades much of the novel. This quality in any work is difficult to describe except by using a metaphor; unfortunately while tropes are admirable in artists, they are usually abominable in scholars. The fictitious Ph.D. whom Nabokov parodies in the introduction makes a number of errors, but when he says that

Humbert can "conjure up a *tendresse*" for Lolita I think he is quite right. HH's memoir makes a very poetic novel.[68] Though he is certainly a grandson of Grandison, there is one part of him which believes to love means to be consumed, to love is to give light with inexhaustible oil. And in spite of the fact that she is usually an annoying, perverse, and conventional brat, seen through the prism of Humbert's adoration, Lolita has "something of angelic light" and becomes one of the most enchanting females of modern fiction. I think it would be impossible to have this feeling for her, without finding Humbert witty—and even truthful, without being more charmed by the poet than repulsed by the pervert.[69] Of course, Humbert's style is often extremely poetic.[70] In this regard the lyrical overture and its fleeting variations all through Part I, serve to establish the dominant musical key of Lolita. Meters, whole lines, separate words and phrases from "Annabel Lee" merge with Humbert's own rhythmic prose to create this special atmosphere, this poetic star and seashell covered backdrop. It is at once a definite and a vague re-evocation of the mysteriously beautiful music of Poe's poem.[71]

Though Humbert and Nabokov love poetry, they sometimes treat it sadistically; their parodies are deft, gleeful, and hilariously awful. "Annabel Lee" is a very serious and beautiful poem. So is *Lolita*, I think. But Humbert's account of *his* Annabel Leigh would certainly strike Poe, mourning Virginia, as a lewd, blasphemous, and unpardonable parody.[72] Humbert's story parallels Poe's in broad outline: it was many a year ago when he was a child and she was a child in a kingdom by the sea when they were in love, and after she died the moon never beamed without bringing Humbert dreams of his beautiful Annabel Leigh—or some

delectable replica of her. The covetous winged seraphs send
a chill wind out of a cloud to take Poe's Annabel, and they
lay her in a tomb by the sounding sea—"Enchantress, fare
thee well!" This is very poetic, but the analogous part of
Humbert's story is perfectly outrageous. A lonely, anonymous pair of sunglasses watch his fruitless efforts to clutch
Annabel's crotch, and, in a kind of dangling syntactical
afterthought, she is knocked off rather than up:

I was on my knees, and on the point of possessing my darling,
when two bearded bathers, the old man of the sea and his
brother, came out of the sea with exclamations of ribald en-
couragement, and four months later she died of typhus in
Corfu. [p. 15]

Thus Humbert sandbags Poe and sentimental readers with a
telescoping one-sentence parody.[73] Of course, all of the allusions and parodies are elements which support the charac-
terization of the narrator himself. They show the quality
and sinister bends of Humbert's imagination, his erudition,
wit, and love of creative destruction.

  Mnemosyne is the heroine of most of Nabokov's work,
and time, the quest and remembrance of time past, is one
of the main themes of *Lolita*. As Nabokov-Humbert re-
creates and re-evokes time in his memoir the reader should
observe and consider the role of cyclicality in the hero's life,
the way certain basic events are repeated, in different
forms, throughout his life.[74] And there are moments of
shock for Humbert when in a blinding flash he becomes
aware of these uncannily recurring acts, characters, and
events.[75] The feeling of *deja vu* overwhelms him. Of course
the archetypal event of Humbert's life is his romance with
Annabel Leigh; this is the dominant theme of his life. He is

usually aware of this himself and often points it out to the reader. But there are subtler variations and parallels on which he makes no direct comment; the reader must make his own memory speak and rely on his own sense of *deja lu* if he is to recognize these. For example, when during his last tryst with Annabel on the Riviera beach he

... had a brief session of avid caresses, with somebody's lost pair of sunglasses for only witness. I was on my knees, and on the point of possessing my darling ... [p. 15]

Later, in his reconstructed Ramsdale diary, he records an erotic lakeside fantasy, an unconscious variation on the Riviera seaside theme:

I was aware that mother Haze hated my darling for her being sweet on me. So I planned my lake day with a view to satisfying the mother. To her alone would I talk: but at some appropriate moment I would say I had left my wrist watch or my sunglasses in that glade yonder—and plunge with my nymphet into the wood. Reality, at this juncture, withdrew, and the Quest for the Glasses turned into a quiet little orgy. . . . [p. 56]

Humbert is unaware of it (at this point, at least), but the idea of a Quest for the Glasses, specifically sunglasses,[76] which becomes a pubertal orgy, occurs as a result of his anguished failure to possess his original darling by the sea. The sunglasses motif has migrated over several thousand miles, twenty-five years, and eight chapters. Humbert's escape from Haze using the quest for sunglasses as an excuse is a deft psychological touch which should make a Freudian gloat, and a brilliant artistic touch which makes the anti-Freudian smile contentedly.

Before dealing with the Viennese delegation one more

Annabel-Lolita parallel has to be quoted. The last Annabel chapter ends:

But that mimosa grove—the *haze* [Dolores Haze, C.P.] of stars, the tingle, the flame, the honey-dew, and the ache remained with me, and that little girl with *her seaside limbs* and ardent tongue haunted me ever since—until at last, twenty-four years later, I broke her spell by incarnating her in another. [p. 17]

There are reverberations of this passage in Humbert's diary. On one occasion he notes: "my darling, my sweetheart stood for a moment near me," that she smelt almost like "the Riviera one," and when she lay down to sunbathe he examined "the swellings of her tense narrow nates clothed in black, and the *seaside of her* schoolgirl *thighs*" (p. 44). Noting these parallels the smug psychoanalyst would conclude that Lolita is obviously a sublimation of Annabel, unconscious ambrosia for Humbert's hairy id. Obviously, says Humbert, but they are wrong. He explains that "in the thralldom of a nymphet the enchanted traveler stands, as it were, *beyond happiness*" (italics in original), and observes:

The able psychiatrist who studies my case . . . is no doubt anxious to have me take my Lolita to the seaside and have me find there, at last, the "gratification" of a life-time urge, and release from the "subconscious" obsession of an incomplete childhood romance with the initial little Miss Lee. [pp. 168–69]

But Humbert assures the doctors (while, please note, again echoing Poe) that he has already had so many delights with Lolita:

. . . that the search for a Kingdom by the Sea, a Sublimated Riviera, or whatnot, far from being the impulse of the subconscious, had become the rational pursuit of a purely theoretical thrill. The angels knew it . . . [p. 169]

In fact, Humbert continues (freely transposing names), his real liberation took place

> . . . at the moment, in point of fact, when Annabel Haze, alias Dolores Lee, alias Loleeta, had appeared to me, golden and brown, kneeling, looking up, on that shoddy veranda . . . [p. 169]

So when Humbert identifies Lolita with Annabel by, for example, recalling, when teaching tennis to Lolita, he "fed ball after ball to gay, innocent, elegant Annabel" (p. 164) we should realize the parallels are consciously contrived, that they are "psychological" only in the purely literary sense, that Annabel is a literary echo, not proof for the theories of the Viennese healers. The only place King Sigmund has in the novel (or any of Nabokov's other works) is in a cage with the *bêtes noires*.[77]

7

Lolita is Humbert's Carmen as well as his Annabel Lee, and he puts Prosper Merimée's *Carmen* to special use. The central character and narrator of Merimée's story is José Lizzarabengoa. It is a simple tale of typical female treachery and typical male foolishness. José falls in love with the gypsy girl Carmen. Carmen is faithful to her own caprice and desire for free expression of her will rather than to any one man or promises, implied or explicit. She then takes up with a Basque picador named Lucas. When she refuses to go away with José he murders her on the spot (knife, two thrusts). Humbert takes this familiar tale, applies it to his own predicament, and misleads unwary readers with strategically placed quotations. We know from the beginning that Humbert is in prison for murder. If Lolita is his Carmen, it is reasonable to suppose that she will be the one to die by Humbert's hand. But the way out of Nabokov's tangle of thorns is not so simple.

In his diary for Wednesday, June 10, 1947,[78] Humbert notes that Lolita played "her favorite 'Little Carmen' record which I used to call 'Dwarf Conductors.' "[79] This song, quoted later, is Nabokov's own invention—with echoes of Merimée and Bizet. On Sunday, June 21 (the summer equinox and, appropriately, a traditional day for pagan orgies in ancient and medieval times) Humbert and Lolita are alone in the Haze living room; Humbert endeavors, surreptitiously and successfully, to relieve himself of his "golden load." The Carmen record plays the accompaniment to his ecstatic self-manipulation and becomes permanently associated with his sexual relations to Lo. During this hilarious scene, reports Humbert:

I recited, garbling them slightly, the words of a foolish song that was then popular—O my Carmen, my little Carmen, something, something, those something[80] nights, and the stars, and the cars, and the bars, and the barmen . . . The stars that sparkled, and the cars that parkled . . . [p. 61]

The song reaches a climax:

. . . I kept repeating chance words after her—barmen, alarmin', my charmin', my carmen, ahmen, ahahamen . . . [p. 62]

Chapter 13 ends with what Humbert remembers of the words of the song, including:

And, O my charmin', our dreadful fights.
And the something town where so gaily, arm in
Arm, we went, and our final row,

> And the gun I killed you with, O my Carmen,
> The gun I am holding now.

(Drew his .32 automatic, I guess, and put a bullet through his moll's eye.) [pp. 63–64]

Later, when Humbert's pistol "Chum" appears—after Lolita-Carmen and he have had "dreadful fights"—the reader is justified in expecting Humbert the murderer will kill his Carmen, put a bullet through his *Doll's* eye. Humbert-José uses a number of allusions to create this expectation. For example, when he imagines Lo leaving him for Hollywood, he says she could end up:

. . . in a dismal ex-prairie state, with the wind blowing, and stars blinking, and the cars, and the bars, and the barmen, and everything soiled, torn, dead. [p. 187]

But this is only a vague hint. Most of the allusions to Merimée occur in Chapters 22 through 29. The series begins when Humbert considers taking Lo to Mexico:

José Lizzarrabengoa, as you remember, planned to take his Carmen to the *États Unis*. [p. 241]

This clearly makes Humbert José and Lolita Carmen. Who is Lucas, the picador, in this little allegory? As Humbert discovered in his search through motel registers, the as yet unknown abductor of Lolita (Clare Quilty) signed himself "Lucas Picador, Merrymay, Pa." (p. 253). The triangle is, it seems, complete and equilateral.

In Chapter 22 there are several gypsy allusions. Lolita is in the Elphinstone hospital; her nurse, Mary Lore, who has "blazing black eyes," is "of Basque descent, as I learned" (p. 243). Humbert inquires of this Basque nurse: "Feeding

my Carmencita well?" (p. 244).[81] And this is followed by a
passage which requires detailed explication:

> "My sister Ann," said Mary (topping information with after-
> thought) "works at the Ponderosa place."
> Poor Bluebeard. Those brutal brothers. *Est-ce que tu ne
> m'aimes plus, ma Carmen?* She never had . . . and I also knew
> the two girls were conspirators, plotting in Basque, or Zemfirian,
> against my hopeless love. [p. 245]

"The Ponderosa place" is where Quilty (alias Gratiano
Forbeson, Mirandola, New York) is staying while plotting,
apparently with the help of the Lore sisters—whom Humbert imagines as gypsies in disguise—to take Lolita away.

Bluebeard, for whom Humbert feels pity and kinship,
was the wife-murdering hero of Charles Perrault's *Barbe
Bleuë* (1697). This is another apparent premonition of
Lolita's death.

"Those brutal brothers" appear on the last page of Perrault's little story for children. As Bluebeard prepares to
decapitate his wife the door bursts open and:

> . . . on vit entrer deux Cavaliers, qui mettant l'épée à la main,
> coururent droit à la Barbe bleuë. Il reconnut que c'étoit les
> frères de sa femme, l'un Dragon et l'autre Mousquetaire . . .[82]

The brothers then skewer the misogynist. Bluebeard's wife's
sister, hollering from a tower, is responsible for getting the
brothers there in the nick of time. The sister's name is
Anne.[83]

Humbert's question in French is lifted right out of
Merimée. Carmen says to Lizzarabengoa: "*J'ai toujours
pensé que tu me tuerais.*" José reports his answer while
telling the tale: "*Carmencita, lui demandais-je, est-ce que
tu ne m'aimes plus?*"[84] Clearly, anyone who knows Merimée's

story is being led to predict Lolita's murder by Humbert. The references continue:

"My Carmen," I said (I used to call her that sometimes) "we shall leave this raw sore town as soon as you get out of bed."
"Incidentally, I want all my clothes," said the gitanilla . . . [p. 246]

An allusion within the allusion provides a new dimension. Humbert says the two girls are plotting "in Basque or Zemfirian." Basque makes sense, because it is a language; but Zemfirian is not. What does this mean? Zemfira is the hot-blooded heroine of Pushkin's *The Gypsies,* a partly narrative, partly dramatic, and very romantic poem published in 1827. In fact it seems that Merimée, who was an early French admirer of Russian literature and translator of Pushkin, took part of the plot for *Carmen* from *The Gypsies.*[85] Unfortunately he made Pushkin's concise, dynamic poem into a long dull piece of prose.

The hero of *The Gypsies* is Aleko, a world-weary exile from St. Petersburg (cousin of René, Childe Harold, Onegin, Pechorin and others) who joins a band of gypsies wandering through Bessarabia. Immediately the gypsy girl Zemfira takes him as her tent-mate. The civilized Aleko imagines he has drunk the milk of Paradise and found freedom and tranquility at last. But after two summers Zemfira's lascivious eyes wander, and more or less secretly she takes a black-eyed gypsy lover, turning cold and unpitying to Aleko. Zemfira's father, a lamb of a man whose wife had left him in a similar manner, counsels Aleko, telling him the moon wanders freely and there's nothing to be done. But unaware that love is not Time's fool, enraged by Zemfira's faithlessness and the way she torments him with mocking, insinuating songs, Aleko trails her to a lewd rendezvous, murders her lover, and when she contemptuously refuses to return with Aleko he kills her too (knife, one thrust).[86]

The triangle "Aleko-Zemfira-gypsy lover" is congruent to the triangle "José Lizzarabengoa-Carmen-Lucas," which (for the moment at least) is congruent to the triangle "Humbert-Lolita-Quilty." Now that the satisfied reader has analyzed the complex layers of allusion and determined that Lolita is the gypsy Zemfira as well as Carmen, he is certain of her fate. Then Nabokov leads him down the last few steps of the garden path to a camouflaged booby-trap.

After three empty years Humbert at last discovers Lo's whereabouts. He heads for Coalmont's "10 Killer Street" with blood in his eye and Chum in his pocket. He continues to tantalize the reader in Chapter 29. First, "fist in pocket" (with Chum), he says: "I could not kill *her*, of course, as some have thought. You see, I loved her" (p. 272, italics in original). But the reader cannot place much trust in this casual "of course" (or in Humbert's announced plan to kill Mr. Schiller); he must still suspect Humbert will shoot Lolita. Love is still the best reason for murder. Humbert says she was:

... still auburn and almond, still Carmencita, still mine; *Changeons de vie, ma Carmen, allons vivre quelque part où nous ne serons jamais séparés* ... [p. 280]

Humbert does not understand that one cannot go back home to romantic love, that where wounds of hate have pierced so deep there can be no true reconciliation. The *quelque part* echoes Quilty's fictitious residence (given in motel registers) "Quelquepart Island."[87] The French appeal

to Lolita is another direct quotation from the final scene of
Merimée's *Carmen:*

*—Changeons de vie, Carmen, lui dis-je d'un ton suppliant.
Allons vivre quelque part où ne serons jamais séparés.* [pp. 69–
70]

But Carmen smiles and refuses. Lolita does too. The parallel
still holds:

NABOKOV

Come just as you are. And we shall live happily ever after.
Carmen, voulez-vous venir avec moi? [p. 280]

MERIMÉE

—Carmen, lui dis-je, voulez-vous venir avec moi? [p. 71]

And in the end:

MERIMÉE

—Tu aimes donc Lucas? Lui demandai-je. (Carmen answers
yes, then no, refuses to go with José, and he murders her.) [p. 72]

NABOKOV

Carmencita, lui demandai-je . . . "One last word," I said in my
horrible careful English, "are you quite, quite sure that . . . you
will not come to live with me? . . .
"No," she said smiling, "no."
"It would have made all the difference," said Humbert Humbert. [p. 282]

At this point Humbert playfully disposes of the clever
readers of Merimée and Pushkin who have been using the

allusions to anticipate the outcome. Instead of murdering Lolita, he pierces the reader's heart with a hyphen:

Then I pulled out my automatic—I mean, this is the kind of fool thing a reader might suppose I did. It never occurred to me to do it. [p. 282]

But it *did* occur to him to make the reader suppose he would. This is one of many deceptions. They occur on several different levels. The masses of disappointed people who read *Lolita* as a dirty book—and even most intelligent readers—will be totally unaware of the literary allusions which Nabokov employs. In this case ignorance is something of an advantage: you cannot be fooled by allusions whose existence you do not even suspect.[88] So Nabokov is deceiving the few readers who do become aware of his devices. And these readers—seeing the elaborate techniques Nabokov uses, already fooled by reversals in the plot (earlier one is led to believe Humbert will murder Charlotte Haze), aware of Humbert's capriciousness, and perhaps familiar with Nabokov's other works—are going to be suspicious from the beginning about the allusions; they will be wary of taking anything for granted. A seemingly unguarded queen may lead to check and mate.

The ultimate deception is this: the eidetic reader will not be fooled by *any* of the allusions—or, at least, he will no longer be fooled when he reaches the end of Chapter 27 (Part II) and sees Dolly's married name: Mrs. Richard F. Schiller. He will, of course, immediately recall that in John Ray's introduction he had read:

Mrs. "Richard F. Schiller" died in childbed, giving birth to a stillborn girl, on Christmas day 1952, in Gray Star, a settlement in the remotest Northwest. [p. 6]

So he knows that, allusions or no allusions, Humbert Humbert will not murder his beloved Lo. The punitive dagger used on Zemfira by Aleko, inherited by Carmen's José, and found along the literary roadside by Nabokov does not end up in the sweet young breast of Lolita.

TWO ▍▌▍ IN QUEST OF QUIMBY-QUIX-QUILTY

You can't imagine, Watson, with what eagerness I listened to this extraordinary sequence of events, and endeavoured to piece them together, and to devise some common thread upon which they might all hang.

THE MUSGRAVE RITUAL

Chapter Two

LIKE some of Nabokov's other novels Lolita is in part a detective story. Nabokov includes and conceals his clues with more than the skill of an Agatha Christie or Maurice Leblanc (two writers alluded to in the memoir). The principal mystery for Humbert and his readers is the identity of the fiend who liberated Lolita on the Fourth of July. Eventually we learn that it was Clare Quilty, the Sade-fancying playwright, author of *The Strange Mushroom, The Hunted Enchanters,* and other works. But when do we make this determination? How do we get through the crystal labyrinth of possible deductions to the one radiant conclusion? On first reading, the reader who, like myself, is not astute will be unenlightened until Chapter 33 of Part II when Humbert finally reveals the secret—and adds a clandestine obscenity:

I had been keeping Clare Quilty's face masked in my dark dungeon, where he was waiting for me to come with barber and priest. "*Réveillez-vous, Laqueue, il est temps de mourir!*" [p. 292][1]

On subsequent readings the humbled reader will pick up the trail of clues which he passed over before; in some cases —the more obvious ones—he will be appalled by his initial blindness, in others—the more devious ones—he will be amazed by Nabokov's craft or intuition and the prodigious demands he makes for complete comprehension.

I propose to follow Quilty's trail through the novel, first reminding *my* readers that by cutting away most of the book and quoting just the clues, I make the pattern Nabokov has woven seem far less complex and delicate than it is within the whole context of *Lolita*. It is not the parts that matter, it is their combinations.

2

Let's start with Humbert's abridged catalogue of the books in the prison library, and the transcription of a page from *Who's Who in the Limelight* for 1946. The passage goes like this:

Quilty, Clare, American dramatist. Born in Ocean City, N.J., 1911. Educated at Columbia University. Started on a commercial career but turned to playwriting. Author of *The Little Nymph, The Lady who Loved Lightning* (in collaboration with Vivian Darkbloom), *Dark Age, The Strange Mushroom, Fatherly Love,* and others. His many plays for children are notable. *Little Nymph* (1940) traveled 14,000 miles and played 280 performances on the road during the winter before ending in New York. Hobbies: fast cars, photography, pets.

Quine, Dolores. Born in 1882, in Dayton, Ohio. Studied for stage at American Academy. First played in Ottawa in 1900. Made New York debut in 1904 in *Never Talk to Strangers*. Has disappeared since in [a list of some thirty plays follows].

How the look of my dear love's name, even affixed to some old hag of an actress, still makes me rock with helpless pain! Perhaps, she might have been an actress too. Born 1935. Appeared (I notice the slip of my pen in the preceding paragraph, but please do not correct it, Clarence) in *The Murdered Playwright*. Quine the Swine. Guilty of killing Quilty. Oh, my Lolita, I have only words to play with! [pp. 33–34]

Now it is often the case that Nabokov will not only provide a clue, but will also emphasize its importance in some way. Here Humbert says the page was "one of those dazzling coincidences that logicians loathe and poets love." The reader, who would probably consider this whole catalogue rather unimportant, will be partially awakened by this remark and decide it must mean the double reference to *The Little Nymph* followed immediately by the name "Dolores" (we know from page one that Lolita, a little-used Spanish diminutive, is Humbert's name for Dolores). The proximity of "nymph" and "Dolores" is a coincidence, but, supposes the reader, a "dazzling" one only in the sick mind of the memoirist. That he is sick in heart and sick in head is confirmed by the apparently fantastic and meaningless biography he provides for Dolores, and by his babbling schizophrenic wordplay. Since Humbert is raving and he says he is only playing with words, one tends to dismiss and forget the entire thing. In fact, however, we are being told at the very outset that Quilty is the one who will be murdered—not any of the Annabels. Examining the *Who's Who* passage on Quilty in retrospect, it becomes clear that most, if not all, of the details given are functional—i.e. they connect to other facts of the novel. These connections are subtle and complex, but they would make it possible for one who remembered all of this passage to deduce the identity of Lo's secret lover. Let me give some examples:

Near the end of the novel Humbert takes Rita, his post-

Lolita flame, to Briceland and The Enchanted Hunters
(the hotel where Lo made Humbert her lover). In search
of lost memories he anxiously peruses the *Briceland Gazette*
for mid-August 1947. He catalogues his reading:

Brute Force and *Possessed* were coming on Sunday, the 24th
to both theaters. Mr. Purdom, independent tobacco auctioneer,
said that ever since 1925 he had been an Omen Faustum [i.e.
Lucky Strike—C.P.] smoker. Husky Hank and his petite bride
were to be the guests of Mr. and Mrs. Reginald G. Gore, 58
Inchkeith Ave. The size of certain parasites is one sixth of the
host. Dunkerque was fortified in the tenth century. Misses'
socks, 39 c. Saddle Oxfords 3.98. *Wine, wine, wine, quipped
the author of Dark Age who refused to be photographed, may
suit a Persian bubble bird, but I say give me rain, rain, rain on
the shingle roof for roses* and inspiration every time. Dimples
are caused by the adherence of the skin to the deeper tissues.
Greeks repulse a heavy guerilla assault—and, ah, at last, a little
figure in white, and Dr. Braddock in black, but whatever spec-
tral shoulder was brushing against his ample form—nothing of
myself could I make out. [pp. 264–265]

This seems to be a chaotic catalogue of trivia, but the lines
I have italicized supply a consequential clue to the identity
of the inebriated and shadowy figure (Quilty) who confronted Humbert on that first visit (pp. 128–129) to The
Enchanted Hunters. Quilty, the *Who's Who* biography informed us, is the author of *Dark Age*. First one must remember this fact. Now compare the quote from the *Briceland
Gazette* to what Humbert's unknown interlocuter said that
August evening in 1947. First the unknown man on the
porch:

"That child of yours needs a lot of sleep. Sleep is a rose, as the
Persians say. Smoke?" [p. 129]

The reader must remember this when, 135 pages later, Humbert reads in the *Gazette:*

Wine, wine, wine,[2] quipped[3] the author of Dark Age who re-fused to be photographed, may suit a Persian bubble bird, but I say give me rain, rain, rain on the shingle roof for roses and inspiration every time. [p. 264]

If one recalls the *Who's Who* passage and connects it to *Dark Age*, the Persians, and roses he can deduce that it was Quilty at The Enchanted Hunters—and this in turn is a vital link to the conclusion that he wrote the *Hunted En-chanters*, the banal drama in which Lolita later plays the lead. A tangle of thorns indeed.

Now let's return to the details of the *Who's Who* biog-raphy and again note:

The Lady who Loved Lightning (in collaboration with Vivian Darkbloom).

This echoes John Ray's introduction where we learn Vivian Darkbloom wrote a biography called *My Cue.* A more im-portant connection is to be made in Part II, Chapter 18, when Lo and Humbert are on the way to Wace. To show how neatly Humbert camouflages his clues I will quote in context:

We spent a grim night in a very foul cabin, under a sonorous amplitude of rain, and with a kind of prehistorically loud thun-der incessantly rolling above us.

"*I am not a lady and do not like lightning,*" said Lo, whose dread of electric storms gave me some pathetic solace.

We had breakfast in the township of Soda, pop. 1,001.[4]

Nothing could be more natural or straight-forward than Lo's remark, but, as you see, it connects to the title in that "boring" catalogue Humbert quoted way back on page 33, and it is therefore conclusive evidence of Lolita's familiarity with Quilty. In fact, Humbert and Lo go to see a Quilty-Darkbloom play in Wace (Lo had been guiding Humbert towards it all along). This must be *Lightning* itself, as is suggested by the reference to a rainbow in it, and the fact that, so far as we know, Quilty and Darkbloom co-authored only one play. Humbert himself gives the authors' names: "I remember thinking that his idea of children-colors had been lifted by authors Clare Quilty and Vivian Darkbloom from a passage in James Joyce" (p. 223).

Moreover he catches a glimpse of the joint authors on the stage and simultaneously remarks it is strange how pleased Lo was with everything, how her new beaming smile appeared. (This special dreamy smile of Lo's first appears when she becomes Q's lover in Beardsley.) He comments to Lo:

"Vivian is quite a woman. I am sure we saw her yesterday in that restaurant in Soda pop."[5]

"Sometimes," said Lo, "you are quite revoltingly dumb. First, Vivian is the male author, the gal author is Clare; and second she is 40, married and has Negro blood."

"I thought," I said kidding her, "Quilty was an ancient flame of yours, in the old days when you loved me, in sweet old Ramsdale."

"What," countered Lo, . . . "that fat dentist? You must be confusing me with some other fast little article." [pp. 223–224]

Humbert lets Lolita get away with an egregious lie here. Had his memory served him better, he would have recalled encountering Quilty as a male, not a female. For one thing, there is a dentist named Ivor Quilty in Ramsdale. Charlotte

says: " 'Dr. Quilty. Uncle or cousin, I think, of the playwright' " (p. 65).⁶ But if we shift back to the Ramsdale
chapters we find even clearer indications. Humbert says
Lo has a picture from a movie magazine over her bed; she
put his initials on it.

Under this was another picture, also a colored ad. A distin-
guished playwright was solemnly smoking a Drome. He always
smoked Dromes. The resemblance is slight. [p. 71]

The drome-smoking playwright's name is not given, but
Humbert does learn it. When he and Lo enter the dining
room of The Enchanted Hunters, they see a lone man in a
sport coat.

"Does not he look exactly, but exactly, like Quilty?" said Lo
in a soft voice . . .
"Like our fat Ramsdale dentist?"
Lo arrested the mouthful of water she had just taken, and put
down her dancing glass.
"Course not," she said with a sputter of mirth, "I meant the
fellow in the Dromes ad."
"Oh Fame! Oh Femina!" [p. 123]

These passages are vital for two reasons: (1) they show that
Humbert had been told that the playwright in the ad was
Quilty (so he was stupid to let Lo tell him Clare was a
female), (2) we have more proof that Quilty was at The
Enchanted Hunters at the same time Humbert and Lo
were. The "Dromes" are mentioned later too, and the reader
should always connect them to Quilty. In the murder scene
Quilty refuses to get serious, and acts moronically manic
when Humbert levels threats and Chum at him. One of
Quilty's nervous (and vegetarian) reactions is: "He kept
taking the Drome cigarette apart and munching bits of it"

(p. 299). Incidentally, "Dromes" are "dromedaries," i.e. Camels. When Humbert fondly imagines Lo as a tennis pro, he fancies "Dolores endorsing a Dromedary" (p. 234); Humbert doesn't realize it, but this is appropriately like her lover Quilty; it is in fact an "unconscious" recollection of the Quilty-Dromes ad over Lo's pristine bed in Ramsdale. This shows Nabokov is a subtle literary psychologist: the Quilty-Dromes-Lolita associations are there in Humbert's demented mind, but he has not yet drawn them together and made the logical deductions. When Lolita does finally tell him it was Quilty there is no surprise—he knew it, he says, without knowing it.

The Dromes ad, the "Persian bubble bird" and the "rain for the roses" all make it possible to conclude that Quilty was at The Enchanted Hunters and was the faceless tippler who spoke briefly and insinuatingly with Humbert on the pillared porch that evening. It is important that we do deduce this; otherwise the conversation between Humbert and Quilty would seem purposelessly mysterious, a sphinx without a secret:

> "Where the devil did you get her?"
> "I beg your pardon?"
> "I said: the weather is getting better."
> "Seems so."
> "Who's the lassie?"
> "My daughter."
> "You lie—she's not."
> "I beg your pardon?"
> "I said: July was hot. Where's her mother?"
> "Dead." [p. 129]

Puns and the coy distortion of words to torment Humbert will later be one of Quilty's favorite games—which he plays in a sinful series of motel registers. If the reader does not know this is Quilty and never figures it out, he will probably take Humbert's interlocuter as just another anonymous pervert. Only a brother pervert would divine Lo was not Humbert's daughter. But as we later learn, Quilty *knew* Lolita and Charlotte in Ramsdale, so he knew Lo was not Humbert's daughter and had good reason to wonder where the devil Humbert got her.

3

Now, the reason it is important to identify this man as the playwright Quilty is that there is a long series of clues connected to The Enchanted Hunters. The trail begins at Beardsley College, when Edusa Gold of the drama department plans a new play and says to Humbert of Lo:

"You just must allow her to take part in *The Hunted Enchanters*. She was such a perfect little nymph in the try-out, and sometime in spring the author will stay for a few days at Beardsley College and may attend a rehearsal or two in our new auditorium." [p. 198]

Humbert finally replies with an obscene *double entendre:* "You win. She can take part in that play. Provided male parts are taken by female parts" (p. 198). And they will be, because Quilty will use the occasion to make Lo his lover.

Quilty's play is about a girl who "imagines herself to be a woodland witch, or Diana" and hypnotizes six hunters "before falling in her turn under the spell of a vagabond poet (Mona Dahl)." Humbert says he noticed the coincidence of the names of the hotel and play, but ascribed it to some common legend or the play suggesting the hotel's name

rather than vice versa—and he decided not to remind Lo
lest she think him mawkish.[7] But after devoting a page to
the subject of the hotel's name—which should be warning
to the astute reader that Nabokov is somehow putting another piece in the multi-colored puzzle—Humbert informs
us that the play was in fact a new one which had just
recently been produced "by a highbrow group in New
York." Then he gives more details about the play.

> ... but a seventh Hunter (in a *green* cap, the fool) was a Young
> Poet, and he insisted, much to Diana's annoyance, that she and
> the entertainment provided (dancing nymphs, and elves, and
> monsters) were his, the Poet's, invention. I understand that
> finally, in utter disgust at this cocksureness, barefooted Dolores
> was to lead the check-trousered[8] Mona to the paternal farm
> behind the Perilous Forest to prove to the braggard she was not
> a poet's fancy, but a rustic, down-to-brown-earth lass ... [p. 203,
> italics in original]

And Diana (i.e. Dolores) probably can prove it if the Vagabond Poet (i.e. Quilty) remains philoprogenitively cocksure.
Poor Humbert! At the time he didn't realize what Lo was
up to, but he makes it possible for the readers of his memoirs
to guess and feel superior to him.

Preparing for the vaguely Maeterlinckian[9] play Lo pre-
tended to be engrossed in problems of expression, "pleading
with me not to come to rehearsals as some ridiculous parents
did" (p. 203). The question arises: Why doesn't she want
Humbert to attend? Remember what Edusa Gold said: the
author of the play would attend some rehearsals. Humbert
recalls one specific occasion:

> There was one very special rehearsal ... my heart, my heart
> ... there was one day in May marked by a lot of gay flurry—it

all rolled past beyond my ken, immune to my memory, and when I saw Lo next . . . I was so struck by the radiant tenderness of her smile that for an instant I believed all our troubles gone. [p. 204]

The gasping, pausing "my heart, my heart" is here only because as he is writing Humbert now realizes (though he didn't then) that after the special rehearsal Lo and Quilty became lovers, and that Lo's new radiant smile is associated with Quilty—and will be associated with him later—at Kasbeam, Champion, and Wace. This brilliant and beautiful passage continues:

"Can you remember," she said, "what was the name of that hotel, *you* know [nose puckered], come on, you know—with those white columns and the marble swan in the lobby? Oh you know [noisy exhalation of breath]—the hotel where you raped me. Okay, skip it. I mean, was it [almost in a whisper] The Enchanted Hunters? Oh, it was? [musingly]. Was it?"— and with a yelp of amorous vernal laughter she slapped the glossy bole and tore uphill, to the end of the street, and then rode back, feet at rest on stopped pedals, posture relaxed, one hand dreaming in her print-flowered lap. [p. 204]

Obviously, Lo has already made the connections which Humbert will not clearly discern until later. But again at the beginning of his next chapter he directs the reader's attention to that remarkable rehearsal, as if to hint there is something for the reader to think about:

(and a week or so after the very special rehearsal Lo had not had me attend) [p. 204]

Then, one Friday soon after, while playing chess with Gaston Godin, he is interrupted by that phone call from Miss Emperor—Lo's piano teacher. She informs him Lo has

now missed two lessons consecutively, Tuesday's and today's. Poor Humbert is aghast. What can Lo be doing? He is
in a daze, his moves become mechanical. In this state of
mind he clumsily loses his queen to Gaston, as Germann
lost to Chekalinsky. I think this is symbolic of losing his
real-life queen, or princess, to Quilty. Symbolically, the
chess queen is Lolita, Gaston is Quilty. During an earlier
game Lo is dancing downstairs and Gaston, says Humbert,
confuses "those distant thuds with the awful stabs of my
formidable Queen" (p. 184). Note also that Humbert "accidentally" calls Gaston "Gustave" just as the phone rings
(p. 204). Gustave Trapp will be one of his mask-names for
Quilty.[10] When Humbert angrily asks Lolita where she was
when she was supposed to be at the piano, she has a felici-
tous excuse:

> ... and said *d'un petit air faussement contrit* that she knew she
> was a very wicked kid, but simply had not been able to resist
> the enchantment, and had used up those music hours—O Reader,
> My Reader!—in a nearby public park rehearsing the magic
> forest scene with Mona. [p. 205]

The "O Reader, My Reader" is Humbert's helpful way of
drawing our attention to Lolita's lie. The "enchantment"
she cannot resist is the enchantment of being in the woods
(or elsewhere) with Mona, alias the vagabond Poet, alias
Clare Quilty, the author of *The Hunted Enchanters*.

Now that Quilty and Dolores are lovers, she determines
to leave Beardsley. In his ignorance of her motives Humbert
is delighted and surprised. Lolita insists that she be allowed
to choose their route—secretly to intersect with Cue's itinerary. Humbert and Lolita are on their way out of Beardsley
when: "We passed the New Hotel, and she laughed" (p.

210). One must suppose the hotel provokes laughter because Quilty had been staying there, and perhaps because she spent some time in his room. Then Edusa Gold drives up beside the Humbert car:

"What a *shame* it was to *tear* Dolly away from the play—you should have *heard* the author *raving* about her after that rehearsal—" "Green light, you dope," said Lo under her breath ... [p. 210, italics in original]

—because she wanted him to get going before Edusa could spill any more potentially explosive beans. Even so, Humbert inquires:

"Who exactly concocted that play?"
"Oh! Yes, of course. Some old woman, Clare Something, I guess. There was quite a crowd of them there."
"So she complimented you?"
"Complimented my eye—she kissed me on my pure brow"— and my darling emitted that new yelp of merriment which—perhaps in connection with her theatrical mannerisms[11]—she had lately begun to affect. [p. 211]

Again Lo gets away with her lies (old woman Clare) and her humor (the kiss on her pure brow). Again the echo ("my darling") of "Annabel Lee," again the vernal yelp of Quilty-connected joy.

4

It all seems so obvious. But when reading the novel it is not. Most of these things can be explained in some other way (much less satisfactory ones as it turns out). Those which the first-time reader cannot fathom can easily be skipped over as "superfluous" novelistic detail, or dismissed as examples of Humbert's queerness; and even those few passages which remain mysterious and seem to require some explanation do not at once fall into an obedient pattern. As M. O. Gershenzon suggested in his analysis of Pushkin's "Station-Master," it is like the picture game of childhood where the puzzle is to pick out the tiger hiding in the foliage—it is difficult to find the tiger, but once you do find it, you wonder how it was you did not see it before. The same is true of Nabokov's pattern. Humbert himself remarks this phenomenon—and in doing so again suggests to us, if we haven't already figured things out, there is a code which we should be deciphering:

I now warn the reader not to mock me and my mental daze. It is easy for him and me to decipher *now* a past destiny;[12] but a destiny in the making is, believe me, not one of those honest mystery stories where all you have to do is keep an eye on the clues. In my youth I once read a French detective tale where the clues were actually in italics; but that is not McFate's way— even if one does learn to recognize certain obscure indications. [pp. 212–213, italics in original]

Some indications are indeed obscure, but some are not—and now that Humbert-Nabokov has disarmed (and warned) his readers with the casual remark about clues in italics—and protesting that his McFate is different—he himself proceeds to put one of the most important clues in italics, so sure is he of his powers of verbal prestidigitation.[13]

The morning after seeing *The Lady who Loved Lightning* in Wace, Lo receives a cabalistic letter from Mona Dahl. Mona says the girl who played Lo's part in *Hunted Enchanters* was fine:

"... but lacked somehow the *responsiveness, the relaxed vitality,* the charm of *my*—and the author's Diana; but there was no author to applaud us as last time . . ." [p. 244, italics in original]

Mona's italicized words are probably quotations from Quilty; the "author's Diana" is Quilty's Lolita. Mona goes on:

"As expected, poor Poet stumbled in Scene III when arriving at the bit of French nonsense. Remember? *Ne manque pas de dire à ton amant, Chimène, comme le lac est beau, car il faut qu'il t'y mène.* Lucky beau! *'Qu'il t'y'*—what a tongue-twister! Well, be good Lollikins. Best love from your Poet [i.e. Quilty. C.P.], and best regards to the Governor. Your Mona." [p. 225]

Humbert comments:

The letter contained an element of mysterious nastiness that I am too tired today to analyze.[14] I found it later preserved in one of the Tour Books, and give it here *à titre documentaire.* I read it twice. [p. 225]

In other words, readers, read it twice—and decode the document. The clue is in italics—and even repeated twice! *Qu'il t'y.* But if you aren't already aware of the pattern and its importance, you will not understand even this clue. And you may be thrown off the track by the whole quotation (and the pun on *beau*), because, as the literary scholar will perhaps see, Chimène is the heroine of Corneille's *Le Cid,* and the French quotation breaks down into two good Alexandrines:

Ne manque pas de dire à ton amant, Chimène,
Comme le lac est beau, car il faut qu'il t'y mène.

Eureka? Not quite. The lines do not occur in Corneille's

play. And there is no parallel between Lolita and Chimène. Why the Alexandrines then? Partly, I suspect, to make the over-studious reader waste his time. Partly as a vehicle and camouflage of the Quilty clue. Lo and Humbert attend the Quilty-Darkbloom play in Wace just before we are given this letter *à titre documentaire,* so that whole hinting passage should remind us of Quilty's name and make it "easier" to see the French *Qu'il t'y* clue.

5

Another link in the chain is forged at Champion, Colorado (Part II, Chapter 21). Humbert is diverted by a fake long-distance call, enabling the devious knave to play tennis with Lolita. Later at poolside Humbert sees the beast half-concealed by trees and notices that peculiar radiant glow on Lo again:

> . . . it dawned upon me that what I had recognized him by was the reflection of my daughter's countenance—the same beatitude and grimace but made hideous by his maleness. [p. 239]

Then Humbert "recognizes" the man as his Swiss cousin, Gustave Trapp. In Humbert's mind Trapp and Quilty are one. This brings us to what might be called the clue of the pigs. Recall Humbert's play on words after the *Who's Who* piece: "Quine the Swine. Guilty of killing Quilty" (p. 34). The word swine is now (in Part II) applied to "Trapp" who in Europe "drank beer with milk, the good swine" (pp. 239–240). Quine the swine is Trapp the good swine—more proof of which can be found by reversing direction again and, in a silent bat-like rush, flying back to The Enchanted Hunters and the "morning after" Humbert raped Lolita—or she him.

The iron gates of life have closed; Lolita is lounging in the lobby. Humbert notes:

A fellow of my age in tweeds . . . was staring at my Lolita over his dead cigar and stale newspaper. [p. 140]

Then he adds: "the lecherous fellow whoever he was—come to think of it, he resembled a little my Swiss uncle Gustave" (p. 141). Then Humbert goes to the desk clerk:

Was pink pig Mr. Swoon[15] absolutely sure my wife had not telephoned? He was. If she did, would he tell her we had gone on to Aunt Clare's place? [p. 141]

"Aunt *Clare*" indeed! Humbert is mocking himself (in retrospect). I don't think this can be looked on as a clue—even with the swine-Trapp-lecher associations in the same paragraph and the theoretical possibility of connecting them to Clare Quilty. Still I suppose one could maintain the word "Clare"[16] by itself—whatever its camouflage—can ring a very small bell somewhere north of the reader's cerebellum.

The next clues come in the catalogue of names from motel registers. The unknown fiend:

. . . could not disguise, no matter how he slanted them, his very peculiar t's, w's, and l's. Quelquepart Island was one of his favorite residences. [p. 252]

This is one of several phonetic clues. We must read "w" for "u"—as in Q*w*ilty. The same principle is used in:

> Que*l*quepar*t I*sland
> Q*ui*mb*y*
> Q*ui*x

When Humbert revisits Briceland with Rita he makes up this poem:

> The place was called "Enchanted Hunters." Query:
> What Indian dyes, Diana, did thy dell
> endorse to make of Picture Lake a very
> blood bath of trees before the blue hotel?[17] [p. 265]

Some of this remains obscure to me, but *Query* is another phonetic disguise of Quilty, and Diana in her dell is Dolly-Lo—earlier, referring to the play, Humbert calls her Diana and uses the phrase "Dolly's Dell" (p. 203).

6

The artistic finesse in the use of phonetic clues is greatest in the scene of Humbert's last meeting with Lolita, when he finally persuades her to reveal who her secret lover, his Nemesis, was:

> Her forehead puckered as in the old bitter days.
> "Not *who?*"
> "Where is he? Quick!" [p. 273]

The "puckering" necessary to make the round owlish sound in *who* (Nabokov's italics) or the "w" in *Qui*ck (my italics), is one of those obscure but very important indications Humbert mentioned earlier. Finally Lo tells Humbert who liberated her, but cruel Humbert does not explicitly tell the reader:

> "Do you really want to know who it was? Well, it was—"
> And softly, confidentially, arching her thin eyebrows and *puckering* her parched *lips*, she emitted, a little mockingly, somewhat fastidiously, not untenderly, in *a kind of muted whistle*, the name that the astute reader has guessed long ago. *Waterproof. Why did a flash from Hourglass Lake cross my consciousness?* I too, had known it, without knowing it, all along.

There was no shock, no surprise. *Quietly* the fusion took place, and everything fell into order, into the pattern of branches I have woven throughout this memoir with the express purpose of having the ripe fruit fall at the right moment... [pp. 273–274]

Quietly, of course, is a phonetic and visual imitation of Quilty; and if the reader puckers his lips and pronounces the name following the detailed instructions Humbert gives he will note that a "kind of muted whistle" is produced—as in the word "waterproof."

Why "waterproof" and the flash from Hourglass Lake? If we turn back to Part I, Chapter 20 when Humbert and Charlotte are at Time-piece Lake we can trace the wrist-watch motif. Recall that Humbert had been almost on the point of drowning Charlotte Haze because he believed they were unobserved and it would be a perfect crime. —But, gutless, he does not murder her. And immediately he learns how "lucky" he had been, because Jean Farlow was concealed in the woods, painting a lakescape, and snoopily watching the Humberts' aquatic antics. Jean says:

"I even noticed something you overlooked. You [addressing Humbert] had your wristwatch on in, yes, sir, you had."

"Waterproof," said Charlotte softly, making a fish mouth. [p. 91]

The mnemosynic flash across Humbert's consciousness when Lolita says "Quilty" (in the peculiar half-mocking, half-fastidious way he describes so carefully) is a phonetic and biological echo of Lo's mother saying "waterproof" in almost exactly the same way, "softly" and puckering, with that pseudo-genteel fastidiousness characteristic of Charlotte. No wonder the similarity makes Humbert shiver. Life's patterns are again repeating themselves. Note that

the name Lolita is contained within Char*lotte,* as Lolita was
carried within Charlotte's body, a fact of life and art to
which Humbert himself draws attention in one of those
outrageous asides:

. . . I would manage to evoke the child while caressing the
mother. This was the white stomach within which my nymphet
had been a little curved fish in 1934. [p. 78]

He observes "biologically this was the nearest I could get
to Lolita" (p. 78). Next he makes Charlotte disentomb pictures of herself ("Lotte") as a child, pictures in which he

. . . was able to make out a dim first version of Lolita's outline,
legs, cheekbones, bobbed nose. Lottelita, Lolitchen.[18] [p. 78]

So the lightning flash across his consciousness reverberates
back through the years to Hourglass Lake, to Charlotte's
white belly with the fish-like Lolita inside, and then back
a generation earlier to Charlotte's own childhood—probably
dating somewhat later than Humbert's seaside love affair
with Annabel Leigh. The whole pattern, biologically and
artistically, somewhat resembles one of those multi-level
pictures in encyclopedias where you lift off page after page
of transparent sheets, each time revealing some new layer
of the anatomy.

7

In the likely event that the reader does not know what
name Lolita gives in that lightning echo of "Waterproof,"
in the event that the pattern does not become clear, the
fruit does not fall, Humbert immediately provides the less
astute readers with more clues—rather obvious ones which

should enable even dullards to deduce Quilty's identity. Lolita says he was practically an old friend, "he had visited with his uncle in Ramsdale," and had spoken at Charlotte's club and kissed Lolita's face:

Did I know he had seen me and her at the inn where he was writing the very play she was to rehearse in Beardsley, two years later? Did I know—It had been horrid of her to sidetrack me into believing that Clare was an old female . . . [pp. 274-275]

Furthermore, the *Wace Journal* had carried his picture (Humbert didn't see it); "the *Briceland Gazette* had not," notes Humbert. Lolita provides even more background information: "Edusa [Gold C.P.] had warned her that Cue liked little girls, had been almost jailed once . . ." (p. 277). —Recall *Who's Who* notes that among Quilty's "hobbies" are "pets." Lolita continues, adding some details on Quilty's own perversions:

"I mean, he had two girls and two boys, and three or four men, and the idea was for all of us to tangle in the nude while an old woman took movie pictures." (Sade's *Justine* was twelve at the start.) [p. 278]

Again, recall the *Who's Who;* one of his three hobbies is "photography."[19] The third hobby is "fast cars," which fits in with the Aztec Red and other machines which follow Humbert and Lo so inexorably.

8

It is certain there are parts of Nabokov's pattern which I have not seen—or, rather, which I have not *recognized* as belonging to the pattern, because we *see* them all. But my point in this chapter, apart from the explications of some of the textual mysteries in *Lolita* and shooting some tigers, has been to give an idea of the kinds of detail a reader of Nabokov must remark and the kinds of logical connections he must make, for poetry is as precise as geometry. Nabokov's works are fabricated piece by piece with the author aware of the exact position in the puzzle of each little piece. The maxim that *dans l'art n'existe pas hasard* is not generally true. But it may be applied to Nabokov's art less figuratively than to the works of most writers. It is one of Nabokov's greatest strengths—and, I think, an ultimate weakness which keeps him from attaining the higher circles of artistic Paradise that some of his nineteenth century Russian predecessors (like Gogol) reached—that he is an extremely clever craftsman. There is an aphorism attributed to the famous Russian general Suvorov which I quote from Prince Vyazemsky's notebooks: "The man everyone says is crafty is not crafty." This might be applied metaphorically, and advisedly, to Nabokov the artist. The secret basis and technique of Gogol's "craft" is so deeply hidden it is almost impossible to say anything critically enlightening about it. But it sometimes appears that Nabokov *thinks* too much, and therefore he can be analyzed. To this statement the great poet would perhaps not subscribe, but, for better or worse, he can still have the last word.

THREE | STYLE

You can always count on a murderer for a fancy style.

LOLITA

Chapter Three

THERE are many people who believe Nabokov is the most brilliant English prose stylist writing today. Conrad (Joseph, not Udo) is the only other writer who has even come close to accomplishing a similar feat, but (apart from the fact he has no place in Polish literature) his ideas and his style are inferior to Nabokov's. The curious fact that Nabokov learned to read English before Russian suggests an inner predilection for the tongue in which he would excel and win fame. Nabokov himself has apologized for his English, saying his command of Russian prose is superior.[1] I don't think that apology was entirely sincere. The lucidity, (sometimes deceptive) simplicity, and euphony of his English are not matched in his Russian. In *Dar (The Gift)* his discursive sentences are so glutted with participial clauses, parenthetical interpolations, and dreary strings of semicolons that it is a chore to cut through them.[2] The contrast between his crystalline English and his conglobate Russian is striking.

Lolita is a first-person narration, so in attempting a formal analysis of the prose one immediately runs into a problem— is the style of the memoir Humbert Humbert's or Nabokov's? The answer is, I think, both. But Nabokov usually dominates. Humbert's voice is the product of a deft ventrilo-quistic trick, with the puppeteer's modified voice still quite recognizable. In fact, some study of the devices reveals that the style of Humbert Humbert strongly resembles the style of John Ray, Jr., the style of the weird and magnificent Commentary to Nabokov's translation of *Eugene Onegin,* and the style of the autobiographical *Speak, Memory.* While it is a thought which I am sure would make Nabokov have ghastly nightmares (related to Humbert's *noctis equi*), a whole book could be written on his style. Since this is vir-tually the first study of his style the goal set is a modest examination of the *sound* of his prose, a few characteristic rhetorical figures, and some aspects of the imagery.

2

Few writers have ever paid more attention to the "instru-mentation" of their prose than Nabokov.[3] Every page of Lolita provides dozens of examples of alliteration and assonance. But Nabokov's style is never meretricious in this respect—as is often the case in the work of more orthodox poets, infinitely less talented people, like Swinburne in England or Balmont in Russia who hide with ornaments their want of art—and if the phonetic combinations ever become amusing, it is because they are supposed to be amusing (Humbert mocks himself occasionally). I have found that even where an epithet appears to have been chosen because of its sound, it usually turns out that pho-netic deftness is complemented by novelty of expression and precision of meaning.

Nabokov's sound play in Lolita runs through the entire phonetic and written alphabet from "*a*brupt *a*ttack" and an

"*a*ctive *A*dam's *a*pple, ogling Lo"[4] to "*z*igzagging *z*anies."[5]
The variety of acoustically coupled epithets is vast. Sometimes it is a simple matter of alliteration on the initial
phoneme:

*a*ging *a*pe, *b*lond *b*itch, *c*olumbine *k*isses, *d*iaphonous *d*arling,
*f*ilthy *f*iend, *g*hastly *g*rin, *h*umiliating *h*assack, *l*imp *L*o, *m*oaning
*m*outh, *p*ubescent *p*ark, *r*aw *r*ose, *s*ubtle *s*pine, *t*ruculently *t*ight,
*v*aguely *v*isualized, *w*elcoming *w*hine

Or the first two sounds may be reiterated:

*bl*azing *bl*ack, *cr*iminal *cr*aving, *di*smal *di*strict, evolving even,
flame-flower, gritty grey, humming hush, loquacious Lo, musk
and the mud, probably protruding, roughly rubbing, scorching
scrawl, tremendous truck, veined vase, whined why

Or the first three:

*bra*sh *bra*ts, *cur*sed *col*onel, *dim*pled *dim*ness, frail frame, gen-
tlemanly generosity, infinitely inferior, limp limbs, perverse
purposes, reports repeated, sorry and sordid, vial of violet-blue,
world of love and work

Or, on occasion, the repetend consists of four or five
phonemes:

comprehending companion, force and foresight, humble Humbert, tortuous and tortoise-slow, strange strain

There are many examples of alliteration on three words in
close succession:

*bl*ackness in the *bl*ue of my *bl*iss, *b*athing *b*riefs and *b*ra; *c*ozy,
*c*oyly *c*overing; *d*readfully *d*istant *d*ays, *f*lorid-*f*aced *f*ellows,
*F*ebruary *f*ooled the *f*orsythia, *g*lobules of *g*onadel *g*low, *h*uge
*h*airy *h*and; *h*umble *h*ushed *h*usband-coach; *l*one *l*ight *L*olita,
predator that prefers a prey

And, in a few cases, four words:

blood bespattered but still buoyant; bones, brains, bronze hair
and blood;[6] driving through the drizzle of the dying day, holding in her hollowed hands, purchases were prompted by the
poignant predilection; release, rearranged my royal robes; with
a wispy, weak, wonderfully; working wonder with one

In the first four groups of examples above I used almost
exclusively adjective-noun combinations. I think these are
the most frequent but there are many other different combinations of parts of speech which could be chosen, which
lend pleasing variety to the prose. Two nouns:

beauty and bride, curiosity and camaraderie, folly and fate,
lodger to lover, magic and might, shams and shamans, vastness
and variety, ox or an ax, pearl and umbra, doubts and pouts

Or two verbs:

banging and booming, grind and grope, grope and hope, loafed
and leafed, lurched and lunged, smile and sway

Noun and verb:

dusk deepened, faces floated, pride prevented, yaps flap

Adverb and verb:

delicately dwelt, falsely fluttering, madly pedaling, primly limit,
roughly rubbing, vaguely visualized

Two adverbs:

deftly and delicately; effusively . . . edusively; serenely and
seriously; smoothly, almost silkily

Or two adjectives (or three):

mobile moist mouth, reliable and bribable, well-tailored white

shorts, wandering and wobbly, stodgy and solemn, brief buoyant bursting "o"

An adverb modifying an adjective:

agonizingly anxious, fadedly feminine, relentlessly radiating,
truculently tight

Verb plus noun as direct object:

adored every pore, bemazed my brain, burn his sweetheart's
buttocks, climb a column

And a variety of prepositional phrases:

basking in the beams, column of onyx, drum in a dream, fiasco
from my foe, litter of light, ordeal of the orb, parody of privacy,
patrimonies of poets, tears of tenderness, teachers in tweeds,
shimmer of shifting

Usually a number of sounds and types are mixed together,
as in these examples:

. . . with geometrical gestures, geographical generalities and
strictly local clues

. . . a plethora of pain that would have hospitalized a Hercules

. . . the *s*ympathetic *s*alts in *F*laubert's *f*ather's *t*imely *t*ear

The instrumentation is ordinarily more complex than a
simple repetition of initial consonants. There are rondo-like
series of repetitions. For example, "polished plop" (p – o –
l – p – l – o – p). Also:

*anim*ated *m*er*k*in, *r*an*k* *a*c*r*es, *s*ecret *t*er*m*inou*s*, un*r*i*p*e *p*ar*t*icle,
*sti*pp*l*ed ar*mp*it

Other kinds of complications are illustrated in the following
sequences of consonants:

su*ppli*ed *pop*lars, *fateful elf, order* and splend*or, gla*nds and
*gang*lia, *vastness* and *variety* of *vistas, ecru* and *ochre, my micro-
scopic script, op*ticle re*plica, inherent sing*ul*ar*ity, re*mem*bered
emb*arra*ssment, au*burn brune*tte

It is almost impossible to compile statistics for such things,
but my subjective impression is that the most common type,
the one which yielded the most examples in my cursory
study, was the type represented by "*motherly mockery.*"
The first and the last sounds of two words are identical. For
example:

blurred blonde, beautiful banal, corrupt and compliant, dan-
gerous Dolores, dropsical dackel, friendly and funny, greenish
gouache, hideous hieroglyphics, hypothetical hospital, lilacs
and lambs, lodger to lover, movieland manhood, parody of
privacy; pharaonic, phallic; pale profile, robed in red, radiant
and robust, ruminated and rumpled, pubescent pet, thwart
theft, venerable vehicle, wiggles and whorls; wind-tortured,
withered; wary . . . weary; wind, witherland; worn woman

The examples given so far illustrate various kinds of (primarily) consonantal instrumentation. Assonance is, I think,
less frequent; and usually it occurs in combination with
alliteration. Assonance becomes particularly noticeable
when consecutive accented vowels are identical. For example:

áwkward dáws, dóubts and póuts, gáudy móth, phóny colónial,
heéded speéd, láughing áthletes, roly-poly Romeo, visionary
Mary, torpid morning, ramshackle castle, dappled Priaps,
dilapidated Appalachian, whirl in a circular skirt, pallid animals, seducing a ewe

Or in these assonant rondoes:

competitive tennis, polished plop, weird interview, rural amours, crumpled mudguard, ugh of disgust, monster of insomnia

Not infrequently alliteration and assonance are combined and there is a repetition of entire syllables in consecutive words, sometimes one short word being entirely repeated and contained in its neighbor. Thus:

articulate art, common concomitant, the course of my correspondence, demure murmur, muffled guffaw, hallucinated lucidity, groveling love, involving . . . voluptas, plumbaceous umbrae, assimilate the simple, strange strain, Dolores said to Mary Lore, commiseration of the camp mistress, newspaper and new pipe, side trips and tourist traps, passport and sport[7]

Given all this hocus-pocus it is not surprising that Nabokov uses many rhymes in his prose:

hail and gale, ox or an ax, as glad as an ad, grope and hope, crimes and pastimes, ads and fads, schemed and dreamed

> The Bearded Woman read our jingle
> and now she is no longer single.
>
> I touched her hot, opening lips
> with the utmost piety, tiny sips . . .
>
> The implied sun pulsated in
> the supplied poplars.
>
> Antebellum homes with
> iron-trellis balconies . . .
>
> Welcome, fellow,
> to this bordello.

My favorite rhyme comes when Humbert thinks he has drugged Lolita with "Papa's Purple Pills" and looks forward

to a furtive orgasm. He says: "My philter had felled her"
(p. 127).[8]

Another kind of instrumentation is one that a linguist—
or someone who speaks Russian—might use and notice.
Nabokov employs combinations of sounds which, phonetically, are very closely related. For example, voiced and
unvoiced pairs of consonants like "b" and "p":

*b*eautiful *b*anal a*pp*le, *l*a*b*oring la*p*, no*b*le ni*pp*le, lim*p* lim*b*s,[9]
va*p*ory vi*b*ration, the *b*almy days and the *p*almy bays, *b*lue *p*lay-
suits, a*b*olished a*pp*le

Or "d" and "t":

li*tt*le ti*dd*le cup, li*tt*le *d*ea*d*ly *d*emon, limpi*d* nymphe*t*, talen*t*ed
impo*t*ent, blin*d* bulle*t*s, *t*echnically *d*eathless, botanist's husband, unlimited delights, Hollywood harlot, utter adoration,
white wide little boys

Less common are alternations of "v" and "f":

com*f*ortably . . . reco*v*ering, *f*ormidable con*v*ertible, sea *v*istas
and smiling *f*aces, stu*ff*ed it with lo*v*e

Or "z" and "s":

de*s*ire and de*c*ision, dangerou*s* desire*s*, da*z*e of du*s*t, di*s*mal dis-
trict, lila*cs* and lam*b*s, fero*c*ious flower*s*, posthumou*s* perfume*s*

There are also sequences of closely related nasals ("m" and
"n"):

*n*umbed her *m*u*mm*y, *m*oan of the *m*orning doves, prim as a
prawn, *m*ute *m*oan of hu*m*an tender*n*ess, se*m*i-a*n*i*m*ated sub-
human

Particularly common are groups of liquids—"r" and "l":

de*l*ightfu*l* debonai*r*, p*r*ovisiona*ll*y p*l*ain, comp*l*ex p*r*ospect, *fluffy* and *frolicsome*, complete with camera, beggar's bliss, prettily plump, permanently eliminate, raffish lass

The day is undoubtedly coming when computers will be used to answer a number of questions about style. I suspect that they are going to show an amazing consistency in the way any given writer uses any given device. I did some rather crude statistical work on similes when writing an earlier book and was surprised to discover that within works as different as *Moby Dick, Crime and Punishment,* and *Dead Souls* the frequency with which similes are used is very consistent. That is, if you count the similes in any two-hundred-fifty-page section there is a strong likelihood that in any fifty-page section you choose there will be about the same number of similes—twenty percent of the total. If this is so, and if one were to do similar studies for a variety of tropes, rhetorical figures, etc. and get the same kind of results—it suggests that in a very real, and mechanical way, that style is the man (or vice versa); it suggests that however individual it might be there is a powerful element of robot-like compulsion in the writing of every man.[10]

Whatever the philosophical speculation and however difficult it is to analyze style, the fact remains that certain rhetorical devices are characteristic of certain writers. For example, no Latin scholar would confuse the rounded periods of Cicero with the irregular sentences of Tacitus. In his love of symmetry and proportion Samuel Johnson uses the devices of parallelism and antithesis with almost mechanical regularity.[11] A reputable Soviet scholar maintains that Chekhov has a marked tendency to use adjectives, adverbs, and verbs in groups of three. And it has been suggested that Tolstoy's prose, particularly his periodic sentences, is characterized by balanced rhetorical arrangements of three—three parallel clauses of one type followed by three of another type with perhaps one containing three parallel prepositional phrases etc.—all in the manner of classical Ciceronian rhetoric.[12]

It is my strong belief that if one computerized *Lolita* one would find that the most common kind of rhetorical-syntactical arrangement involves "two's" rather than "three's." Nabokov is addicted to balanced pairs, to verbal twins—some fraternal, some identical, and some even Siamese. I am going to call these "doublets" and subdivide them into various types, depending on the kind of repetition, parallel, or antithesis in each. One typical kind of doublet involves a repeated word and semantic parallelism:

> half a haunch and half a shoulder
>
> shared secrecy and shared guilt
>
> dream dad protecting his dream daughter
>
> normal big males with normal big mates
>
> an absolutely perfect imitation of absolutely top-notch tennis . . .
>
> in so many *cabanes* in so many beech forests
>
> upon a succession of balconies a succession of libertines toasted the bliss of past and future nights . . .

Reverse mirror images are created by the doublets in which the two halves are antithetical:

> good lands and bad lands
>
> beastly hot or blindingly cold
>
> cold anger and hot tears

sad eyes up, glad eyes down

the man of law and the man of water

the portion of hell and the portion of heaven

hot little Haze informed big cold Haze

to gartered black sock and sloppy white sock alike

the present day log cabin boldly simulating the
past log cabin . . .

finis my friends, *finis* my fiends

Now it is very often the case that these doublets are partially
"sound-determined." Phonetic structure as well as syntactical structure plays a role in maintaining the neat
balance between the two sides. Alliteration makes the
parallelism more noticeable and more pleasing:

. . . on the *pr*omise*d* beach, in the *pr*esume*d* forest

In the *gl*ove compartment—or in the *Gl*adstone bag . . .

. . . *bl*essed by the local priest and *bl*oated with drink

. . . *l*ight of my *l*ife, fire of my *l*oins

My *s*in, my *s*oul.

. . . gentle *J*ohn and dewy-eyed *J*ean[13]

The *c*orpuscles of *Kr*ause were entering the *ph*ase of
*fr*enzy . . .

. . . above the tribulations of ridicule, beyond the possibilities of
retribution

. . . from beaches which were either too bleak when lone or too
populous when ablaze

. . . a guided trip along a bridle trail

I had stolen the honey of a spasm without impairing the morals
of a minor.

. . . to the Mexico border, to mythical bays

. . . in my dimness of thought, in my darkness of passion

Other sonorous doublets:

> logicians loathe and poets love
>
> coach in French and fondle in Humbertish
>
> ineffectual wipers and whimsical brakes
>
> crisp echoes and Electra's cries
>
> her dramatic drives and lovely volleys
>
> of the noble nipple and massive thigh
>
> the fragile child of a feminine novel
>
> my masked lust to her guileless limbs
>
> morbid cerebration and torpid memory

A few "with" doublets:

with fitted bodice and flared skirt

with parlor books and period furniture

with a scrunch and a skid

with its many sidetrips and tourist traps, secondary circles and skittish deviations . . .[14]

Plus a chastely beautiful doublet structured on parallel dactylic adjectives modifying parallel trochaic nouns:

> with cinnabar nipples and indigo delta

And, appropriately, rhyming pairs:

"I think you stink."

The stars that sparkled and the cars that parkled . . .

. . . and the swirls at the sides and the curls at the back . . .

Valechka was a Schlegel, and Charlotte a Hegel . . .

Longer sets of doublets with complications:

. . . through the musk and the mud, through the dirt and the death . . .

. . . chiaroscuro of smiles and frowns, doubts and pouts . . .

. . . the car and the dog and the sun and the shade and the wet and the weak and the strong and the stone . . .

. . . from counter to counter, from rock ledge to seaweed, and the belts and the bracelets . . .

. . . harangues of hers where entreaty and insult, self-assertion and doubletalk, vicious vulgarity and childish despair, were interwoven in an exasperating semblance of logic which prompted a semblance of an explanation from me . . .

Given Humbert's passion for puns and parallels, the zeugma becomes almost inevitable:

Humbert . . . burning with desire and dyspepsia.

. . . listen to receding girl laughter in between my heart throbs and the falling leaves

. . . my hindwheels only whined in slosh and anguish

And a final example which in rhetoric and sentiment suggests Pope's *The Rape of the Lock:*

A change of environment is the traditional fallacy upon which doomed loves, and lungs, rely.[15]

I have saved for last the examples which I think really clinch the case that Humbert's phrases are often "sound-determined." Alliteration is the invention of children, the passion of admen and madmen; so it is fitting for Humbert to record combinations like "Papa's Purple Pills," the "C's" of his fantasy Camp Q ("Canoeing, Coranting, Combing

Curls"), or the "D's" of Beardsley School ("Dramatics, Dance, Debating and Dating"), and to mention the girdle which "trims tums, nips hips." I think it is manifest that phonetic considerations were paramount in the choice of epithets like those in the following phrases:

Trappish moustache, transparent taupe socks, pristine armpit, Javanese gestures, perfunctory underthings, plumbaceous umbrae, leaving the livid house, provide . . . provisional plates[16]

"Provisional plates" is perhaps the best example, because dentures are always called "temporary," not "provisional." Or consider plangent doublets like these:

sparrows sperm or dugong dung

doleful days in dumps and dolors

maroon morons near blued pools

glacial drifts, drumlins, and gremlins and kremlins . . .

. . . and pouted, and dimpled, and romped, and dirndled

Another proof that the style is sound-determined is the way certain nouns or adjectives inevitably attract modifiers containing closely related sounds, just as certain atomic particles always fall into the proper orbits. Appropriate and euphonic epithets like "perfect impunity" and "trim turf" are used more than once (trim turf also decorates the *Onegin* Commentary, III, 144). With "golden" we find other "g's" and "l's": golden giggle, golden goal, golden load. "Pubescent" is one of Humbert's favorite adjectives—usually it is harmonically combined, as in:

pale pubescent girls, pubescent park, pubescent concubine, pubescent pet, perfect pubescent figure, bemused pubescent girls

Then there is the nymphetry:

nymphic echo, limpid nymphet, nimbleness [of] nymphet, limp nymphet, every inch of their nymphancy, nymphets imitate, mythopoeic nymphet

The lilt of Lolita's name (and Humbert's affectionate insanity) determines the words which usually surround it: loved, beloved, live, lust, limbs, legs, little, lap, lively, lovely, lassie. Thus we find:

Lo's legs, behold said Lo, compliant Lolita, ivory full of Lolita— full of the feel, frail Lo, little Lo, Loquacious Lo, Look said Lo, limp Lo, lovely lap [of Lo], little Lo's; Lo, little limp Lo; Lo a lollipop, blasé Lo, Lo's lovers, lulled by Lo, Lolita's length, listening to Lo, Dolly-Lo however lagged, Lo ludicrously, lone light Lolita, Lo . . . languidly left; Lolita, pale and polluted; living Lolita
   Dolores endorsing a Dromedary, Dolly's Dell, doted on Dolly, Dolly's day adjacent, delightful Dolly, dolorous . . . darling

As shown above, similar games are played with Humbert's double name.

3

Proper names present almost unlimited possibilities to the writer with an alliterative ear. He can choose any existing name or combination of names, and he can contrive entirely new ones. For example, Humbert invents:

Bryan Bryanski, Sullen Sullivan, Reverend Rigger, Richard Roe, Dorothy Doe, Gaston Godin, Maurice Vermont and Marion Rumplemeyer, Cecilia Dalrymple Ramble, Vanessa van Ness, Leslie and Louise, John and Jean, Marion and Mabel, Onyx and

Eryx (lakes), Glance and Gulp (a magazine), and A Deceitful Seatful (a bar)

But the foundations of Humbert's pseudonymry are not entirely phonetic. Some of the names are bilingual puns: Dr. Blanche Schwarzmann (White Blackman), Avis Byrd[17] (bird bird), Pavor Manor ("dread" or fear and trembling manor—Quilty's house).[18] Some names, as Humbert suggests, are projections of his own emotions and hostilities—Killer St., Dick Skiller, Hunter Rd., Grimm Rd. Some are metonymical or synecdochical versions of his own first perception of a person. Thus Mrs. Opposite (who lives opposite Haze), Mr. Taxovich (who drives a taxi), the Junks (Mr. is a junk dealer), and Jutting Chin (a comic-strip detective—Dick Tracy I suppose). Some of the names have meanings even in English (Darkbloom, MacCrum, Miss Cormorant). Others, in one language or another, suggest certain basic functions of the human anatomy in the general area of Uncle Toby's monstrous wound: Lake Climax, Conception Park, D. Orgon, Harry Bumper, Miss Redcock (mentioned in connection to a lipstick and urinal), Miss Lebone, Laqueue, Quimby, Dr. Kitzler, etc. Miss Lester and Miss Fabian, two spinster professors, live together; anagrammatically their names spell: Les-bian.

There are literary allusions: Dr. Byron, Shirley Holmes (Conan Doyle), Dr. Tristramson (Lawrence Sterne's Tristram Shandy), Vanessa van Ness (an allusion to Jonathan Swift's presumed lover, *E*sther *Van*homrigh, known as Vanessa). The cleverest of these allusions are the names Electra and Edusa Gold. Edusa Gold teaches drama at Beardsley School; Electra is her sister. In Sophocles' *Electra* the heroine's sister is named Chrysothemis, which means literally "the golden law."

Finally, to return to the question of sound-determination, some names seem to have been chosen just as balls for verbal ping-pong:

As to the cot—

"Mr. Potts, do we have any cots left?" Potts, also . . . would see what could be done.

"However—would there be a spare cot in 49, Mr. Swine?"

"I think it went to the Swoons," said Swine.

Gee, Ed, that was bad luck—referring to G. Edward Grammar . . .

"Phil calls Philadelphia, Pat calls Patagonia."

. . . I (King Sigmund the Second) said Boyd was quite a boy.

4

Nabokov is an admirer of Gogol, Andrey Bely, and James Joyce. Humbert shares his opinion of the sublime Dubliner and is mad besides, so various kinds of verbal distortion, puns, and neologisms are entirely appropriate in his memoir. Here is an example of this verbal self-entertainment:

. . . denying by implication that she denies those amusing rumors, rumor, roomer . . .

In another case Beardsley becomes Birdsley and Humbert drunkenly imagines the "address Bird School, Bird, New Bird." A Joycianly macaronic passage occurs in Part I, Chapter 27, when Lo undressed her gentle limbs

And lay down in her loveliness.

Hesitant Humbert is confusedly over-desirous, and as a result, to the oneirologist his behavior, and the whole scene, have an uncanny dreamlike quality:

Seva ascendes, pulsata, brulans, kitzelans, dementissima. Elevator clatterans, populus in corridoro. Hanc nisi mors mihi adimet nemo! Juncea puellula, jo pensavo fondissime, nobserva nihil quidquam . . . [p. 122]

Latin has got mixed up with its romantic descendants and run wild, so Humbert burns for his maid of rushes. Among other things, this is one way to disguise touchy subjects (*kitzelans*).

The huge number of puns makes it impossible to present more than a few illustrations of various types. For example, people familiar with the parks in the Dakotas will get the point when Humbert and Lolita travel from the Northwest to the East "across good lands and bad lands." Anyone will feel the verbal twist when soldiers rape women in a "sad, sacked village." One separate category is composed of puns constructed on a metamorphosing repetend:

[Charlotte grew up] like a fakir's fake tree.

[Mabel wears a] halter with too little to halt.

[Humbert buys] pumps of crushed kid for crushed kids.

[Beale's father unconscious on the lawn is] a banked banker so to speak.

[The dead playwright is a] quilted Quilty.

The names Dolores, Haze, and Lolita give rise to several plays on words:

"I spend my doleful days in dumps and dolors. We (mother Haze, Dolores and I)"

Lolita is his "dolorous and hazy darling." He mentions the "healthy heat which like summer haze hung about little Haze."

"And Lo and Behold, upon returning, I would find the former..."

" 'Lo,' cried Haze . . . 'And behold,' said Lo (not for the first time) ..."

And when Dolores disappears in Wace, Humbert says, "There was no Lo to behold." There are, as I have noted, puns on other names too. Two more examples are Humbert's reference to his "own cumbersome sins" (i.e., Humbertsome sins) and his designation of the pursuing fiend (who reminds him of his Uncle Trapp) as "merely a trapped flatus."

This leads to the delicate topic of *double entendre*. I suspect that the outraged congressmen and nervous mamas who thought *Lolita* was a dirty book missed most of these, but the device is used with pleasantly erotic regularity. For example, Humbert deplores the Mann Act "as lending itself to a deplorable pun" and declares that, "Among Sicilians sexual relations between a father and his daughter are accepted as a matter of course" (intercourse, of course). He reads a book with the "unintentionally Biblical title *Know Your Own Daughter.*" In the same region he implores Lo to "leave your incidental Dick and this awful hole." A typical drama teacher's question is "where are the climaxes in *Love under the Lindens,*"[19] and Humbert permits Lo to participate in the *Hunted Enchanters* "provided male parts are taken by female parts"—and they are, Quilty's by Lo.

The lexical range of Lolita is extremely broad—extending from the slang used by Lo (and picked up by Humbert) through parodies of advertising jargon, to dialect words like "girleen" and rare concatenations like "bi-iliac crests" (for dorsal cheeks)—and a generous Gallic sprinkling of French phrases and words. Humbert-Nabokov's stylistic proclivity is to prefer an uncommon polysyllable to a common monosyllable ("ambulate" instead of "walk"), rare words to ordinary ones (he uses "nictating" for "winking" and when he describes vertical shadows under the eyes he goes to the moon for a word and calls them "plumbaceous umbrae"). His style is extremely periphrastic; in his effort to avoid commonplace expressions he resorts to metaphor—and the result is sometimes faintly ridiculous. Thus when a character reaches under a table she is "dipping her hand into the nether anatomy of a lamp table." On another occasion Lolita "became aware of the bananas on the table and uncoiled herself tableward."[20]

There are not as many neologisms in the novel as anyone who has not spent many diverting hours reading dictionaries will probably think. Most of the neologisms are the result of an extra suffix or the welding together of two words (there may be one or two joints), as in:

blackground, bubbleblood, cryptochroism, daddum, gagoon, gnomide, honeymonsoon, kiddoid, lakescape, libidream, mauve-mail, Proustianize, pseudolibido, solipsize, spoonerette, strum-string, truckster

Compound words of a more temporary nature (because they are hooked only by a hyphen) are also used:

clenched-teeth, dove-dull, dusk-brimming, dusk-mellowed,

gravel-groaning, sweet-moaning, Lo-less, plush-and-plate,
putty-buff-and-snuff, quip-quoted, giggle-chat

5

So far as I know no one has yet invented a good scheme
for analyzing the rhythm of prose, but it is necessary to say
a few words on the subject regarding *Lolita*. Even writers
less gifted than Nabokov are aware that sometimes an epithet, for example, may be perfect in terms of meaning and
phonetics but not be *juste* rhythmically, because for some
usually unanalyzable reason the sequence of accents it creates simply does not sound right—and that they must find
another epithet which will fit as precisely as the last missing
piece fits into a puzzle. This principle extends from epithet
to clause to sentence to paragraph. If we look through the
admirably short list of Nabokov's favorite prose writers we
will find the names of Chateaubriand, Gogol, Bely, Joyce,
and Proust—all of whom wrote prose which is universally
recognized as being rhythmical. Bely even experimented
with metered prose—a device which Nabokov briefly copies,
by way of experiment only, in his Russian novel *Dar*. And,
in a book which Nabokov has praised in his own book on
Gogol, Bely attempted to analyze Gogol's prose rhythm.

One elementary device which is commonly used to create rhythmic effects is a figure of repetition—anaphora,
epiphora, epizeuxis, etc. These rhetorical figures create the
most basic kinds of parallelism. A figure used frequently in
Lolita is synathrismus[21] (the "heaping figure"). For example:

dancing, falling, daisying
fidgeting, shuffling, scraping

twitching, shivering, smirking

sprawling and sobbing and pinching

panting, scrambling, laughing, painting

explanations, demonstrations, ullulations

fussily, busibodily, cunningly

madly, clumsily, shamelessly, agonizingly

sweetest, simplest, gentlest, dumbest

pushed her, pinched her, prodded her

lovely, truthful, dreamy, enormous

hot, happy, wild, intense, hopeful, hopeless whisper

In the last example Humbert parodies himself and perhaps the ardent romantics who have always been fond of this figure.

One rarely finds entire prose passages which conform to any one regular metrical pattern, iambic, dactylic, or whatever. But one can find *some* clauses or sentences in almost any prose that do fit a pattern. The unsolvable problem has been to develop a way to analyze every line and compile statistics which would prove that writer N's prose is more rhythmical than writer G's prose. So we are left with our subjective impressions and the possibility of citing a few examples to support them—which is what I intend to do now. It seems to me that sometimes there can be no mistaking the conscious effort to create rhythm. Take, for example, Charlotte's remark to Humbert:

That was my Lo . . . and these are my lilies.

The rhythm is enhanced by the initial alliteration in the

accented words: *That . . these/Lo . . . lilies.* It is a beautiful sentence, one of those which literary epicures can mentally repeat, savoring the sounds. Other examples? Humbert has taught Lolita to play tennis, and following her serve:

to pátter úp at ónce tó the nét

on her nímble, vívid, white-shód feét.

The sequence of vowels in the last four words from the high short "i" to the long closing "e" is somehow the perfect progression. The sequential patter of "t's" and "p's" on the palate and lips echoes the opening lines of the novel— and Lo's footsteps on the court.

Among the sentences which have caught my attention the most frequent rhythms are ternary, usually anapestic:

My schéme wás a márvel óf prímitive árt.

The Párk wás as bláck as the síns it concéaled.

. . . and my sénses were súddenly fílled to the brím.

. . . but nót out óf sight ón the pópulous párt of the *pláge*.[22]

And nów comes the póint of my pérfect-críme párable.

I had áctually seén the ágent of fáte.

. . . in a kínd of fictítious, dishónest, but éminently satisfáctory seáside arrángement . . .

. . . were stárred and spáttered by vénemous béasties and swépt by húrricane wínds.

I fáked ínterest

by bringing my head so close

that her hair touched my temple

and her arm brushed my cheek

as she wiped her lips with her wrist.

. . . in the wind, in the pollen and dust, a flower in flight, in the

beautiful plain as descried from the hills of Vaucluse.

The lyrical overture to *Lolita* is one of the most rhythmic passages in the novel. There is a filmed television interview with Nabokov during which he reads the opening lines, first in English, then in Russian. The contrast is striking—partly because of the change in rhythm, and partly because the stepping English tongue stumbles over some harsh Russian sibilants. —Incidentally, the interview is fascinating, because Nabokov's whole manner and personality seem to change when he takes up the book to read. During most of the interview he appears to be nothing more than a quiet, quaint, benign old man who, as he is the first to point out, doesn't talk very well. He often hesitates or lapses into trivialities, and he is somewhat ill at ease.[23] But when he picks up *Lolita* he is immediately transformed; Lolita gives him confidence, and his voice is forceful as he reads the opening lines:

Lolita,

light of my life,

fire of my loins.

My sin, my soul.

Lo-lee-ta:

the tip of the tongue

taking a trip of three steps down the palate

to tap, at three, on the teeth.

She was Lo, plain Lo, in the morning,

standing four feet ten in one sock.

She was Lola in slacks.

She was Dolly at school.

She was Dolores on the dotted line.

But in my arms she was always Lolita.

The passage is as brilliant phonetically (the "e's" and "i's" with the "t's" and "th's") as it is rhetorically and rhythmically. It is an extraordinary accomplishment; he has accurately described the movements of the tongue when the heroine's name is pronounced (with a Russian dental "t" rather than the English alveolar one), while simultaneously melting in allusions to "Annabel Lee," and introducing us immediately into the peculiarly ecstatic world of his pervert-narrator's idolatrous mind.

6

The nature and quality of a writer's imagination frequently reveals itself in the kind of imagery which he uses, and reading several of Nabokov's novels—ones written over a span of three decades and in two different languages—I have been struck by the way certain kinds of images and certain ways of *making* images are used repeatedly. I say "struck," but that is rather misleading for initially it is rather that one becomes vaguely aware of repeated images without seeing the pattern clearly and being able to define generic types of repetition to discover any of the basic principles and formulas which Nabokov characteristically uses. For example, when reading *Lolita,* although I am not one of those readers who has constant visual reactions to literature, I had the feeling that if I were an artist there would be distinct patterns of shade and color suggested by the imagery which could be put on a canvas as a "typical" landscape of *Lolita.* Then I began marking passages "typical imagery"—though I wasn't really aware why in each case I did so. But a few clearly discernible groups of images did emerge when the file cards had been shifted and arranged. The largest of these groups was made up of "sun and shade" images:

... I dissolved in the sun, with my book for fig leaf, as her auburn ringlets fell all over her skinned knee, and the shadow of leaves I shared pulsated and melted on her radiant limb . . . [p. 22]

... and, wobbling, they [two girls on a bicycle] slowly, absently, merged with the light and shade, Lolita! Father and daughter melting into those woods! [p. 86]

As I look back on those days, I see them tidily divided into ample light and narrow shade . . . [p. 34]

The reflection of the afternoon sun, a dazzling white diamond with innumerable iridescent spikes, quivered on the round back of a parked car. The leafage of a voluminous elm played its mellow shadows upon the clapboard wall of the house. Two poplars shivered and shook. [p. 47]

Lolita had been safely solipsized. The implied sun pulsated in the supplied poplars; we were fantastically and divinely alone;

I watched her, rosy, gold-dusted, beyond the veil of my controlled delight. [p. 62]

. . . but in her eyes it vied in beauty and animation with the sun and shadows of leaves rippling on the white refrigerator. [p. 79]

From my window, through the lacquered shiver of poplar leaves, I could see her crossing the street . . . [p. 91]

A station wagon popped out of the leafy shade of the avenue, dragging some of it on its roof before the shadows snapped . . .[24] [p. 75]

I knew the sun shone because my ignition key was reflected in the windshield . . . [p. 97]

When, through the decorations of light and shade, we drove up to 14 Thayer Street . . . [p. 178]

[Lo on a bike] . . . and press her tongue on one side of her upper-lip and push off with her foot, and again sprint through pale shade and sun. [p. 190]

There he stood, in the camouflage of sun and shade, disfigured by them . . . [p. 239]

. . . she saw our joint account as one of those southern boulevards at midday that have solid shade on one side and smooth sunshine on the other . . . [p. 79]

. . . still nothing might have happened, had not precise fate, that synchronizing phantom, mixed within its alembic the car and the dog and the sun and the shade and the wet and the weak and the strong and the stone. [p. 105]

When the passages are thus arranged in sequence, the reasons for that inchoate impression of visual consistency can be seen clearly. The *landschaft* of *Lolita* is drenched in sunlight, reminiscent of some impressionist paintings, dappled canvasses of dazzling light and fuzzy shade. The sun-drenched setting of the novel stretches chronologically and longitudinally from the brilliant beaches of the Riviera to the hot pointillistic poplar leaves shimmering and melting in New England, to the blazing Western plains and deserts which Lo and her dad cross in their humble blue car.[25] Of course, as an old poet has said:

> The sun, which yearly melts the polar ice,
> Has quite the opposite effect on vice.

It is a fact not too often discussed that writers control the weather in their fictional worlds. In *Lolita* rain falls rather rarely. It seems to be premonitory when it does. Not long after the Aztec Red pursuer appears (in Chapter 18) Humbert and Lo

. . . spent a grim night in a very foul cabin, under a sonorous amplitude of rain, and with a kind of prehistorically loud thunder incessantly rolling above us.

Darkness and rain seem to be associated with Quilty, sunlight with Annabel Haze. At The Enchanted Hunters Quilty is hidden in the dark when he talks to Humbert; at poolside in Champion he stands in the shadows watching Lolita swim. When Humbert drives down Grimm Rd. to Quilty's Pavor Manor the first time all is "dank, dark, dense, forest,"[26] and the next day when Humbert goes to kill Quilty, "A thunderstorm accompanied me most of the way back to Grimm Road . . ." However the pattern is broken, for by the time he arrives at Quilty's the sun is visible and "burning like a man."

Another group of metaphors and comparisons used in

Lolita is taken from photography and movie-making. Often this imagery is connected to the theme of memory. For example:

If I close my eyes I see but an immobilized fraction of her, a cinematographic still, a sudden smooth nether loveliness . . .

I could have filmed her! I would have her now with me, before my eyes, in the projection room of my pain and despair!

. . . a performance that had affected her as little as if she were a photographic image rippling on a screen . . .

I seemed to have shed my clothes and slipped into pajamas with the kind of fantastic instantaneousness which is implied when in a cinematographic scene the process of changing is cut.

In the selenian glow, truly mystical in its contrast with the moonless and massive night, on a gigantic screen slanting away among the dark drowsy fields, a thin phantom raised a gun, both he and his arm reduced to tremulous dishwater by the oblique angle of that receding world—and the next moment a row of trees shut off the gesticulation.

In the course of the evocations and schemes to which I had dedicated so many insomnias, I had gradually eliminated all the superfluous blur, and by stacking level upon level of translucent vision, had evolved the final picture.

Such visual effects are characteristic of Nabokov's writing in general. I suspect he favors photographic images (no pun intended) because they are: (1) artificial pictures of life—not "real," (2) colored or colorable, (3) limited by some kind of frame—so that one's mental eyes are focused on a relatively small, circumscribed surface. These conjectural "reasons" require some explanation.

Art, according to Nabokov, does not deal with the realm

of "messages" or "real life" at all. It is a special abstract realm of nonutilitarian delight, a refined world of intricate patterns the connections and symmetries of which writers— and some readers—see. Art is as potentially perfect as a jig-saw puzzle or a chess problem; it is a "game of intricate enchantment and deception,"[27] a game played by the artist as he transforms his memories into a tangible object which in its way is as abstract, limited, self-contained and perma- nent as a photograph, a frozen segment of remembered time. And in Nabokov's novels these moments re-evoked and frozen by means of words are usually re-evoked in tech- nicolor. Nabokov, as he explains in *Speak, Memory,* has col- ored hearing. The obsession with colors in his novels and critical works has always annoyed me, so I was happy to discover there was some basic physiological cause for it. He tends to judge writers on the basis of the way they use colors—so that in commentaries on everything from *The Song of Igor's Campaign* to *A Hero of our Time* we find him riding this polychromatic hobby-horse and harping about the dull or brilliant use of colors.[28] He is somewhat less concerned with color in *Lolita* than in, say, *Speak, Memory;* but the number of hues used is still prodigious. And for the word-painter re-evoking past time the colors are connected to the theme of memory. Thus:

I notice I have somehow mixed up two events . . . but such suffusions of swimming colors are not to be disdained by the artist in recollection. [p. 265][29]

A particularly beautiful example contains a clear echo of Pushkin:

Through the darkness and the tender trees we could see the

arabesques of the lighted windows which, touched up by the colored inks of sensitive memory, appear to me now like playing cards ... [p. 16]

This echoes a metaphor connecting memory and cards in *Eugene Onegin* (VIII, XXXVII). When he tries to read, Eugene is distracted by memories of the past, "secret legends of the heart's dark ancientry," as Nabokov translates:

> And by degrees into a lethargy
> of feelings and of thoughts he falls,
> while before him Imagination
> deals out her motley faro deck.

In the Commentary Nabokov refers to this as "one of the most original images of the novel" (p. 228) and "the magnificent image of the faro game" (p. 229).

The third characteristic of the photographic image is the circumscribed area. Reading Nabokov, it seems to me his typical imagery is a highly detailed description of what one sees inside some fairly small focus or frame—created by a window, mirror, or other glass object; a telescope, microscope, or stereoscope; or by any flat surfaces which reflect light (again in colors, often flashing prismatically) such as water, polished furniture, metallic objects, lacquered or other glossy objects. These reflection-images usually involve complex designs and patterns, often described in geometrical terms.[30] For example, when Humbert tries to remember a license-plate number:

What remained of it in my mind were the initial letter and the closing figure as if the whole amphitheater of six signs receded concavely behind a tinted glass too opaque to allow the central series to be deciphered, but just translucent enough to make out its extreme edges. [p. 228]

Watery surfaces appear repeatedly. Humbert's knees feel like reflections of knees on the surface of rippling water (p. 42), and:

A breeze from wonderland had begun to affect my thoughts, and now they seemed couched in italics, as if the surface reflecting them were wrinkled by the phantasm of that breeze. [p. 133]

In my chess sessions with Gaston, I saw the board as a square pool of limpid water with rare shells and stratagems rosily visible upon the smooth tesselated bottom, which to my confused adversary was all ooze and squid-cloud. [p. 235]

If we apply the chess-art comparison again, Nabokov takes the place of Humbert, the Reader the place of poor Gaston trying to see the bottom through the ooze and squid-cloud.

The delicacy and complexity of Nabokov's metaphors is amazing and satisfying. For example, "Possibilities of sweetness on technicolor beaches had been trickling through my spine . . ." (p. 38). When one analyzes the metaphor, it becomes apparent the word "trickling" is used because *sand* (from the beaches) trickles—as well as because of its quintuple phonetic echo (t-r-i-k-l) of "technicolor." Similarly, when Humbert, thinking of sleeping pills for the Hazes, says, "a delicately allied, pharmacopeial thought did tinkle in my sonorous and clouded brain" (p. 73), the "tinkle" in his brain is an echo of the pills dropping into a glass. Nabokov is also master of vivid tactile metaphors ("Cold spiders of panic crawled down my back" p. 142), humorous metaphors ("Moth holes had appeared in the plush of matrimonial comfort" p. 29), and a vast variety of pun-filled sexual ones ("The conjuror had poured milk, molasses, foaming champagne into a young lady's new white purse; and lo, the purse was intact" p. 64).[31]

Nabokov's similes are usually original, but even with the unexpected juxtapositions, they tend to be less memorable than his metaphors. His touch is sometimes delicate:

Mrs. Haze gently touched the silver on both sides of her plate, as if touching piano keys . . . [p. 65]

. . . Lo's little belongings that had wandered to various parts of the house to freeze there like so many hypnotized bunnies. [p. 83]

But more often he goes in for the comic, with various grotesqueries, sometimes half-beautiful:

. . . a kind of gown that makes thin-armed teenagers look like flamingoes. [p. 188]

. . . the dog started to lope alongside my car like a fat dolphin. [p. 282]

sometimes not:

Her lips were like large crimson polyps. [p. 106]

[Charlotte] had awoke at once, as fresh and strong as an octopus. [p. 96]

She lit up and the smoke she exhaled from her nostrils was like a pair of tusks. [p. 196]

. . . a row of parked cars, like pigs at a trough. [p. 119]

I was as limp as a toad. [p. 248][32]

The images are frequently more complex than polyps or toads. There are places where two similes come together in concert with metaphor:

The fatal gesture passed like the tail of a falling star across the blackness of the contemplated crime. It was like some dreadful silent ballet, the male dancer holding the ballerina by her foot and streaking down through the watery twilight. [pp. 88–89]

A rather rare device (for Nabokov or anyone else) is the use of a triple-vehicled simile—with one tenor:

My next bullet caught him somewhere in the side, and he rose from his chair higher and higher, *like old,* gray, mad Nijinski, *like Old* Faithful, *like some old* nightmare of mine, to a phenomenal altitude . . . [p. 304]

Even rarer is the use of four conjoined vehicles:

. . . our poor romance was for a moment reflected, pondered upon, and dismissed like a dull party, like a rainy picnic to which only the dullest bores had come, like a humdrum exercise, like a bit of dry mud caking her childhood. [p. 274][33]

One really has to feel sorry for old Humbert at this point; it is a moment of infinite melancholy, Humbert could well think life is a romantic message scribbled in the dark by someone's anonymous shade (compare *Pale Fire,* lines 235–36, and the *Onegin* Commentary, III, 145). But as he often points out, Humbert is a poet—only a poet would write such a passage. And only Nabokov would be incapable of playing it straight all the way through—note the pun: "a humdrum exercise" should also read "a Humbert exercise."

7

There are several other features of the style of *Lolita* I would like to comment upon briefly. The dialogue is often presented without narrative interpolations, without "stage directions." Tolstoy, to go to the opposite extreme, rarely lets his characters say more than a few sentences without commenting at length on the facial reaction and gestures of his interlocuters, on the fine shades of tone used by each speaker, on any small changes in position, and on the inner motives and thoughts of each. Nabokov tends to present a series of speeches as a single "block" with no explanations until after the characters finish (or before they start).[34] Even verbs of saying ("Look out," *Lo yelped*, etc.) are employed sparingly. One result is that the reader must follow very carefully or he will lose track of who is speaking.

A very interesting kind of transition is illustrated by the following passage:

> I set out two glasses (to St. Algebra? to Lo?) and opened the refrigerator. It roared at me viciously while I removed the ice from its heart. Rewrite. Let her read it again. She will not recall details. Change, forge. Write a fragment and show it to her or leave it lying around. Why do faucets whine so horribly? A horrible situation, really. The little pillow-shaped blocks of ice—pillows for polar teddy bear, Lo—emitted rasping, crackling, tortured sounds as the warm water loosened them in their cells. [pp. 98–99]

First there is a transition to interior monologue in the parenthetical questions ("to St. Algebra? to Lo?"). Then note the shift from past tense narration to present tense interior monologue after the second sentence. Jumbled telegraphic sentences and isolated verbs convey the confusion in Humbert's mind as he reacts to Charlotte's discovery and deciphering of his secret diary. After "really" there is a transition back to ordinary narration—but with an interpolated question of something once said to or by Lolita (the polar teddy bears). Incidentally, Humbert, like many of Nabokov's other heroes, has a somewhat schizophrenic way of referring to himself in the third person. For example:

Humbert was perfectly capable of intercourse with Eve, but it was Lilith he longed for. [p. 22]

The widower, a man of exceptional self-control, neither wept or raved. He staggered a bit, that he did; but he opened his mouth only to impart such information or issue such directions as were strictly necessary . . . [p. 100]

In the latter case Humbert is giving a parody of a newspaper account which, along with his madness, provides explanation of the shift from first to third person. Elsewhere Humbert mentions that he has made changes in his memoir for purely artistic reasons—this could also account for these occasional shifts in narrative person.

Humbert's syntax is sometimes unintentionally shaky.[35] He says "then put back Humbert's hand on the sand" (p. 91) rather than "put Humbert's hand back on the sand." Note the clumsy position of "in a minute" in this sentence:

I am going to pass around in a minute some lovely, glossy-blue picture-postcards. [p. 11]

Or the vagrant "anyhow" in this one:

Valechka—by now shedding torrents of tears tinged with the mess of her rainbow make-up—started to fill anyhow a trunk, and two suitcases . . . [p. 31]

Other examples:

To Dr. Blue, who by then was stroking my hand, I spoke in tears of the liquor I bolstered too freely a tricky but not necessarily diseased heart with. [p. 249]

Lo at the time still had for the cinema a veritable passion . . .
[p. 172]

Going back to the lobby, I found there a change . . . [p. 128]

One syntactical device which is highly characteristic of
Nabokov's style is what I would term the "parenthetical
non-sentence." For example:

My very photogenic mother died in a freak accident (picnic,
lightning) when I was three . . . [p. 12]

. . . I cast around for some place in the New England country-
side or sleepy small town (elms, white church) where I could
spend a studious summer. [p. 37]

A related device is used in this sentence:

But how his heart beat when among the innocent throng, he
espied a demon child, *"enfant charmante et fourbe,"* dim eyes,
bright lips, ten years in jail if you only show her you are looking
at her. [p. 22]

Note that after the French phrase (an allusion I haven't
identified), the syntactical logic breaks down; "with" or
"she has" is omitted before "dim," and "you will get" is
omitted before "ten." Of course, here as elsewhere the device is used consciously. The elliptical concision is, to use a
partly Gogolian phrase, admirable in all respects.

8

There is more, much more, that can and probably will
be written about *Lolita.* Humbert's use of French, the structure and composition of his Ramsdale diary, and his various
poems all deserve attention. There are many themes and
motifs which I have not traced in this essay. For example,

Humbert makes love to Annabel Leigh in the garden by "Roches Roses"; on the double bed in room 342 of The Enchanted Hunters where Lo deflowers him there is "a Tuscan Rose chenille spread." In the same room Lolita fills the mirror "with her own rosy sunshine"; Humbert calls her his "rose-darling," and those nymphets around her "Lolita's handmaids and rosegirls"—among these are Mary Rose Hamilton and Rosaline Honeck, the "bodyguard of roses" surrounding her name in the Ramsdale class list, and Eva Rosen, her nymphet friend in Beardsley. So far as I am aware no one, even those who believe *Lolita* is a piece of pornography, has observed the hints (see, among others, pages 183–84, 191) which make it clear that Gaston Godin is a happy homosexual who, like Virgil's sheepherders, undoubtedly prefers a lad's peritoneum to Humbert's delicious *fillettes.*

I am tempted to say a few words about Humbert's character and Lolita's, but as Nabokov himself has pointed out (in his introduction to Lermontov's *A Hero of our Time*) such analyses are worthless to anyone who has read the book. Suffice it to say that Humbert is at once a lucky idler, a man of many sighs, a priest who worships only beauty, a creature stepping out from behind the stove dressed in the clothes of a traveling scholar, a poet who by immortalizing Lolita proves that Pushkin's Mozart is not entirely correct when he says:

> Genius and crime are incompatible,
> Two worlds apart.

Like a "character-study" a commentary on subjects mildly satirized in the book—middle-class ladies, teen magazines, movies, motels, girls' schools, summer camps, car colors, newspapers, hitchhikers, tour books, tourist maps, science, psychiatry, and modern sex education, to name only a few— would be pointless. Nabokov's acerbic attacks on books with Morals and Messages are well-known, if not completely well-founded. It is somewhat ironic that he preaches his view of art so insistently that he becomes one of the most tendentious of writers. This is not meant as criticism, for I think it is clear he is one of the very best writers of this century. In order to mirror the book-length epanalepsis of his novel, those who are interested should begin and end their perusal of this study with a careful reading of *Lolita.*

Characteristic Imagery

The following passages from five works contain some of the imagery which led to the generalizations made in Chapter III (Section 6).

. . . he saw, with that quick smile with which we greet a rainbow or a rose, a blindingly white parallelogram of sky being unloaded from the van—a dresser with mirror across which, as across a cinema screen, passed a flawlessly clear reflection of boughs, sliding and swaying not arboreally, but with a human vacillation, produced by the nature of those who were carrying this sky, these boughs, this gliding facade. [*The Gift*, p. 14]

But the years roll on, and honor is no consolation; recollections either melt away or else acquire a deathly gloss, so that instead of marvelous apparitions we are left with a fan of picture postcards. Nothing can help here, no poetry, no stereoscope—that gadget which in ominous bug-eyed silence used to endow a cupola with such convexity and surround mug-carrying Karlsbad promenaders with such a diabolical semblance of space that I was tormented by nightmares after this optical diversion far more than after tales of Mongolian tortures. [*The Gift*, p. 26]

. . . some kind of vision danced before his eyes—like a thousand iridescent needles of light that surround the dazzling reflection of the sun in a nickel-plated sphere . . . [*Invitation to a Beheading*, p. 73]

It seemed as though at any moment, in the course of his movements about the limited space of the haphazardly invented cell, Cincinnatus would step in such a way as to slip naturally and effortlessly through some chink of the air into its unknown coulisses to disappear there with the same easy smoothness with which the flashing reflection of a rotated mirror moves across every object in the room and suddenly vanished, as if beyond the air, in some new depth of ether. [*Invitation to a Beheading*, p. 121]

He listened sleepily, clasping his knees and looking at a chink of lacy light between the loosely closed curtains, through which a gaslamp from the street shone lilac-tinged white. From time to time a faint glimmer sped over the ceiling in a mysterious arc and a gleaming dot showed on the desk—he did not know what: perhaps one facet of a paperweight in the guise of a heavy crystal egg, or a reflection in the glass of a desk photograph. [*The Defense*, p. 37]

The veranda cast a black triangular shadow on the bright sand. The avenue was paved with sunflecks, and these spots, if you slitted your eyes, took on the aspect of regular light and dark squares. An intense latticelike shadow lay flat beneath a garden bench. The urns that stood on stone pedestals at the four corners of the terrace threatened one another across their diagonals. [*The Defense*, pp. 56–57]

A hot, torpid expanse of cement and sun lay beyond the geometrical solids of various clean-cut shadows. [*Pnin*, p. 17]

One way to do it might be by making the scenery penetrate the automobile. A polished black sedan was a good subject, especially if parked at the intersection of a tree-bordered street and one of those heavyish spring skies whose bloated gray clouds and amoeba-shaped blotches of blue seem more physical than the reticent elms and evasive pavement. Now break the body of the car into separate curves and panels; then put it together in terms of reflections. These will be different for each part: the top will display inverted trees with blurred branches growing like roots into a washily photographed sky, with a whalelike building swimming by—an architectural afterthought; one side of the hood will be coated with a band of rich celestial cobalt; a most delicate pattern of black twigs will be mirrored in the outside surface of the rear window; and a remarkable desert view, a distended horizon, with a remote house here and a lone tree there, will stretch along the bumper. [*Pnin*, p. 97]

It was a pity nobody saw the display in the empty street, where the auroral breeze wrinkled a large luminous puddle, making of the telephone wires reflected in it illegible lines of black zigzags. [*Pnin,* p. 110]

I saw a city, with its toylike trams, linden trees and brick walls, enter the compartment, hobnob with the mirrors, and fill to the brim the windows on the corridor side. [*Speak, Memory,* p. 95]

A bronze angle, a surface of glass or polished wood here and there in the darkness, reflected the odds and ends of light from the street, where the globes of tall street lamps along its middle line were already diffusing their lunar glow. Gauzy shadows moved on the ceiling. [*Speak, Memory,* p. 54]

On the white windowsills, on the long window seats covered with faded calico, the sun breaks into geometrical gems after passing through rhomboids and squares of stained glass. [*Speak, Memory,* p. 67]

Although it was still broad daylight, our cards, a glass and, on a different plane, the locks of a suitcase were reflected in the window. [*Speak, Memory,* p. 94]

In the purity and vacuity of the less familiar hour, the shadows were on the wrong side of the street, investing it with a sense of not inelegant inversion, as when one sees reflected in the mirror of a barbershop the window toward which the melancholy barber, while stropping his razor, turns his gaze (as they all do at such times), and, framed in that reflected window, a stretch of sidewalk shunting a procession of unconcerned pedestrians in the wrong direction, into an abstract world that all at once stops being droll and loosens a torrent of terror. [*Speak, Memory,* p. 225]

It occupied a very small sector of the enormous sky and had the peculiar neatness of something seen through the wrong end of a telescope. [*Speak, Memory,* p. 151]

. . . what loveliness the glass slides as such revealed when simply held between finger and thumb and raised to the light—translucent miniatures, pocket wonderlands, neat little worlds of hushed luminous hues! In later years, I rediscovered the same precise and silent beauty at the radiant bottom of a microscope's magic shaft. In the glass of the slide, meant for projection, a landscape was reduced, and this fired one's fancy; under the microscope, an insect's organ was magnified for cool study. [*Speak, Memory,* p. 118]

. . . I see the awakening of consciousness as a series of spaced flashes, with the intervals between them gradually diminishing until bright blocks of perception are formed, affording memory a slippery hold. [*Speak, Memory,* p. 3]

A Calendar of Lolita

1910

Humbert Humbert born in Paris.

1911

Clare Quilty born in Ocean City.

1919

June: A canary flies through Humbert's house at the same time one flies through Annabel Leigh's house.

1923

June–August: Annabel Leigh *(mère de souvenirs)* and Humbert on the Riviera.
September: Humbert goes to the lycée in Lyon.
December: Annabel dies in Corfu.

1933

Lolita's brother born (two years before the Haze-Becker marriage).[1]

1934

April: Lolita engendered in Vera Cruz by Harold Haze and Charlotte Becker Haze (honeymoon trip).

1935

January 1: Lolita (Dolores Haze) born in Pisky.
April: Humbert's brief affair with Monique. Shortly after this he marries Valeria Zborovski.

1937

Lolita's brother dies.

1939

Humbert is divorced by Valeria. He receives an American inheritance.

1939–40

Winter: Humbert lives in Portugal.
Spring: Humbert comes to the United States. Quilty writes *The Little Nymph.*

1940–42

Humbert works on a history of French literature for English-speaking students.

1943–44

Humbert in an insane asylum.

1944

Summer: Lolita stays with Miss Phalen in California.

1944–45

Humbert accompanies an Arctic expedition. Valeria Maximovich dies (childbirth) in California.

1945

November breathed with Autumn chill and the Hazes moved to Ramsdale from Pisky.

1945–46

Humbert's fanciful report on the expedition is published in the *Annals of Adult Psychophysics*.

1946–47 (May)

Humbert in an insane asylum.

1947

May 30–June 3: Humbert arrives in Ramsdale and meets the Haze girls.

June 4 (Thursday): He begins his diary.[2]

June 9 (Tuesday): Licks a speck from Lo's eyeball.

June 20 (Saturday): Ends diary.

June 21 (Sunday): Tangles with Lo on the couch. She is unaware of his orgasm. Simultaneously, Charlotte is in church praying for Humbert's love and the Lord's guidance.

June 23 (Tuesday): A shopping trip.

June 25 (Thursday): Angry Charlotte drives Lolita to Camp Q. Humbert rushes into Lolita's bedroom and sniffs the crotch of her pants. Later he accepts Charlotte's proposal.

End of June: Humbert marries Charlotte Haze.

July 29 (Sunday): Leslie seen bathing naked by Jean Farlow.[3]

July 31 (Tuesday): Humbert almost murders Charlotte at Hourglass Lake.

August 7 (Tuesday): Charlotte receives a letter from the second Miss Phalen.

August 8 (Wednesday): Charlotte reads the diary, and she is killed by Beale's swerving auto.[4]

August 13 (Monday): Lo goes hiking.

August 15 (Wednesday): Humbert leaves Ramsdale and picks up Lolita.[5] They spend the night at The Enchanted Hunters in Parkington. Clare Quilty is also staying there.

August 24 (Sunday): "Brute Force" and "Possessed" come to the movie-house in Parkington.

1947–48

August–August: The first cross-country trek from NE to SE to SW to NW to NE to 14 Thayer St., Beardsley.

1948

November (last week): Lo sighs frequently in class.

December (a Monday before Christmastime): Headmistress Pratt talks to Humbert about Lo's sexual backwardness and persuades him to let her participate in a play, *The Hunted Enchanters.*

Christmas: Lo has bronchitis.

1949

January 1 (Saturday): Humbert gives Lo a new bicycle for her fourteenth birthday.

May 20 (approximately): Clare Quilty attends a special rehearsal of *The Hunted Enchanters* and begins to lure Lolita into his orbit.

May 24 (Tuesday): Lo misses her piano lesson.

May 27 (Friday): Lo misses another lesson; Miss Emperor calls Humbert to inquire why.

May 29 (Sunday): Humbert and Lo leave Beardsley, meeting Edusa Gold on the way out of town.

June 7 (approximately): They drive to Chestnut Court in Kasbeam. There Quilty has a rendezvous with Lo while Humbert is being barbered. Humbert notices the Aztec Red pursuer in the days which follow (it was kept in a garage at the motel).

June 10–14 (approximately): In mid-June they attend *The Lady Who Loved Lightning* in Wace, catching sight of Clare Quilty and Vivian Darkbloom.

June 14–25 (approximately): They proceed to Champion, Colo. by way of Snow. In Champion Humbert is diverted by a fake phone call; Quilty plays tennis with Lo. Later by the pool, infantine Lolita frolics in an Aztec Red swimsuit for Quilty's delectation. Humbert vomits.

June 27 (Monday): Arrival at Silver Spur Court, Elphinstone, Colo. Lo is ill, enters the local hospital.

June 29–30: Lo begins reacting like a darling to the healing serum.

July 2 (Saturday): Humbert visits Lo bringing a load of gift books he had driven sixty miles for—and sees an envelope (from Quilty) crested "Ponderosa Lodge."

July 3 (Sunday): Humbert falls ill and cannot go to the hospital.

July 4 (Monday): Shortly after 2:00 P.M. Lo checks out with Quilty.

July 5–November 18: Humbert searches "342" motels between Ponderosa Lodge and Beardsley.

Winter: Lo, who has left Quilty, is working in restaurants.

1950

January 1: Humbert sends Lolita's year-old bicycle and other things to a home for orphaned girls on the Canadian border. Shortly afterward he enters a madhouse where he stays until May.

May: Humbert picks up Rita.

1951

September: Humbert begins a stint as visiting scholar at Cantrip College.

1952

June: Humbert ends his stay at Cantrip, gets Rita out of the local jail.

August: He revisits Parkington with Rita (for the second time), looks up newspapers for mid-August, 1947.

August–September: Charles Holmes killed in Korea.

September 18 (Thursday): Lolita mails a letter requesting money from her dad.[6]

September 22 (Monday): HH receives the letter, leaves Rita with a note taped to her navel.

September 23 (Tuesday): Humbert confronts Lo and her husband Dick Schiller in Coalmont. She tells HH it was Quilty, refuses to leave with him.

September 24 (Wednesday): Humbert returns to Ramsdale, finds out Quilty's location from Clare's Uncle Ivor.

September 25 (Thursday): Humbert Humbert murders Clare Quilty (first degree) with a .32 automatic and is arrested for reckless driving.

November 16 (Monday): Humbert dies of coronary thrombosis.[7]

December 25 (Thursday): Dolores Schiller dies in Gray Star, a settlement in the remotest Northwest.

Notes

1. Vladimir Nabokov, *The Gift* (New York: Popular Library, 1963), p. 211.

2. Vladimir Nabokov, "On a Book Entitled *Lolita*," *Lolita* (New York: Putnam's Sons, 1955), p. 313. This edition is used for all quotations from the novel.

3. Vladimir Nabokov, *Invitation to a Beheading* (New York: Capricorn Books, 1965), p. 7.

4. After I completed my manuscript, Professor Boldino observed that I had failed to follow my own advice here. This is the explanation: Nabokov says the quotation he gives in *Invitation to a Beheading* is from "the author of *Discours sur les ombres*." And *Discours sur les ombres*, we learn in *The Gift* (pp. 348–49), was written by "the French thinker Delalande." And Delalande, and his dates (he lived one year longer than Chateaubriand), and the *Discours*, and the quotation about the novel, and the novel, are Nabokov's fabrications! As he notes in the foreword to *Invitation to a Beheading*, the only author who influenced him was "the melancholy, extravagant, wise, witty, magical, and altogether delightful Pierre Delalande, whom I invented" (p. 6).

5. Vladimir Nabokov, *The Defense* (New York: Popular Library, 1964), p. 219.

6. Later Humbert mentions that the abductor checked out of his motel on July 4, and that his own search began on July 5. These are further indications for the reader.

7. Immediately after presenting the list Humbert hints that

"mask" is the key-word for understanding it. I haven't been able to interpret this clue, so I don't know all the games Nabokov is playing with the list.

8. The change from "z" to "s" occurs in both of the editions I own; it is apparently just a proofreading error. Phyllis Chatfield, another class-list name, is mentioned in the same scene.

9. In his book on Gogol, for example, he uses a different spelling of Auver (the doctor who killed Gogol) each time it occurs, and in an appendix to the translation of *Onegin:* "Abram (Avram, Avraam, Ibragim) Petrovich, or Petrov (baptismal patronymic) Annibal, or Gannibal, or Ganibal (assumed surname), hereafter referred to as 'Abram Gannibal' " . . . (*Eugene Onegin,* Vol. III, p. 391).

10. There is a curious verbal echo in the medieval story of Lancelot of the Lake. Lancelot approaches the "Dolorous Gard," where "at the foot of the rock on one side ran the Humber, and on the other flowed a great stream." See *Sir Lancelot of the Lake,* trans. L. A. Paton (New York, 1929), p. 141. —An allusion to the "Dolorous Tower" in one of Nabokov's short stories led me to this.

11. This is an allusion to Poe as well as Joyce. See below, section six.

12. Suggestive of *Lolita* is this passage: ". . . A is for Anna like L is for liv. Aha hahah, Ante Ann you're apt to ape aunty annalive! Dawn gives rise. Lo, lo, lives love! Eve takes fall. La, la, laugh leaves alasss!" *Finnegans Wake* (New York: The Viking Press, 1965), p. 293.

13. James Joyce, *Ulysses,* 7th impression (London: The Bodley Head, 1955), p. 470. Also, this passage from *Ulysses:*

Ben Jumbo Dollard, rubicund, musclebound, hairynostrilled . . . shaggy-chested shockmaned, fatpapped, stand forth, his loins and genitals tightened into a pair of black bathing bagslops. [p. 495]

is reminiscent of Nabokov's description of Quilty:

. . . the wool on his chest spread like a symmetrical trophy, his navel pulsating, his hirsute thighs dripping with bright droplets, his tight wet black bathing trunks bloated and bursting with vigor where his great fat bullybag was pulled up and back like a padded shield over his reversed beasthood. [p. 239]

14. Humbert registers in 342 motels, he says. Perhaps, but the Haze house (where he meets Lolita) is at 342 Lawn Street and it is in room 342 of The Enchanted Hunters that he first makes love to her.

15. Even though a second and careful reading will reveal that there are more than enough clues for one to have deduced Quilty's identity, it is doubtful whether at this point in the first reading many people will have solved the mystery.

16. Laurence Hanson, *The Life of S. T. Coleridge—The Early Years* (New York, 1939), p. 260.

17. Wilhelm Reich, *The Discovery of Orgone* (New York: The Orgone Institute, 1942).

18. A "Reverend Thomas Morell" had written the caption under a photograph hanging over Lo's bed—next to Quilty's photo. See p. 71.

19. See below, section seven.

20. See above, footnote 14.

21. Apart from this, a town called "Shakespeare," an elusive comment on Polonius (p. 152), and some comments on *King Lear* (p. 267), there are two other direct allusions to Shakespeare. Lo and Mona Dahl practice a scene from *The Taming of the Shrew* together (p. 193). Humbert is not specific, but Act II, scene I is the only one the girls could do alone. Lo would play Katharina, and Mona Bianca. Elsewhere Humbert alludes to Romeo and Juliet, asserting Romeo was rather fat in spite of all that "snow" and "joy juice" (meaning, I suppose, the "dope," the various potions and poisons).

22. When Lo is in the hospital Humbert gives her a copy of Browning's *Dramatic Works*. Incidentally, in Kinbote's commentary to line 347 of *Pale Fire* I find the following uretic allusion to Pippa (vowels reversed):

This was the spot where the good farmer invariably stopped, and once, when they happened to be accompanied by his little boy, the latter, as he trotted beside them, pointed and remarked informatively: "Here Papa pisses."

23. I take it is pure coincidence or convention that "Roland Pym" precedes Clare Quilty in the *Who's Who* which Humbert reads in

prison (p. 33), and that E. A. Poe's *Narrative of A. Gordon Pym* begins:

My name is Arthur Gordon Pym. My father was a respectable trader in sea-stores at Nantucket, where I was born. My maternal grandfather was an attorney in good practices . . .

and *Lolita* (minus the marvelous prefatory piece) begins:

I was born in 1910, in Paris. My father was a gentle easygoing person, a salad of racial genes. . . . His father and two grandfathers had sold wine, jewels, and silk, respectively.

24. *Ulysses*, p. 239, p. 243. There are several other references to things Ormond.

25. Compare *Pale Fire*, lines 641–42:

> Fra Karamazov, mumbling his inept
> *All is allowed*, into some classes crept . . .

26. Humbert gives Lo a copy of Andersen's "The Little Mermaid." The tale's combination of poetry and savagery must appeal to the poet-monster. He would no doubt like little Lolita to enchant him with the same ultramundane devotion shown by the fifteen-year-old mermaid in love with the handsome prince. Following her death the mermaid becomes a "daughter of the air" for three hundred years. She is told:

Unseen, we fly into the homes of men, where there are children, and for every day on which we find a good child who pleases his parents and deserves their love, God shortens our days of trial. . . . But if we see a naughty, mischievous child we must shed tears of sorrow, and each tear adds a day to the time of our trial.

Humbert is obviously trying to tell Lolita something.

27. The suggestive lines Humbert quotes on page 49:

> Un petit mont feutrée de mousse délicate,
> Tracé sur le milieu d'un fillet escarlatte

are the eleventh and twelfth of Belleau's *Impuissance* ("*Quel desastre nouveau, quel estrange malheur*"), which contains some quite indelicate descriptions slightly censored in *L'Enfer des Classiques,* ed. Pierre Dufay (Paris, 1942), pp. 56-58.

28. When, stunned, Humbert returns to Silver Spur Court knowing Lolita has left him, the moonlight creates premonitory shadows:

> I made out what looked like the silhouette of a gallows on what was probably a school playground . . . [p. 243]

This is reminiscent of a detail from the nighttime ride of Lenore and her lover in Bürger's ballad. In his Commentary on *Onegin* (III, 154), Nabokov quotes some famous lines and notes: "At one point (st. XXV) they pass by a gibbet in the stark moonlight." (Also, see below, page 141.) —Incidentally, the shadow is probably cast by a basketball goal. That Humbert should see a gallows shadow on a playground is a fine "symbolic" touch.

29. At the beginning of Part II (Chapter 1) Humbert alludes to Flaubert in this way:

> We came to know—*nous connûmes,* to use a Flaubertian intonation—the stone cottages under enormous Chateaubriandesque trees [found in *Atala* and *René,* C.P.], the brick unit, the adobe unit, the stucco court, on what the Tour Book of the Automobile Association describes as "shaded" or "spacious" or "landscaped" grounds.

The next two paragraphs begin "*Nous connûmes.*" Both contain catalogues relating to the travels of Humbert and Lolita. This appears to be a play on the opening paragraph in the penultimate chapter of *L'Éducation sentimentale.* It deals with Frédéric's travels:

> Il voyagea.
> Il connut la mélancholie des paquebots, les froids réveils sous la tente, l'étourdissement des paysages et des ruines, l'amertume des sympathies interrompues.
> Il revint.

30. Humbert's ecstatic description of his first night alone with Lo is a paraphrase of a passage from the Nickspub scene of *Finnegans Wake:*

> Then she crept into my waiting arms, radiant, relaxed, caressing me with

her tender, mysterious, impure, indifferent eyes . . . Endearing was she . . .
[p. 122]

Then flamebird lindy so tigrislikely creepkissed into Sopwith's attendring
arms radiant relaxed rebullient caressime conmystering impurring hello-
helloing bluegoldeyes. Endeafied ami. [*Finnegans Wake*, 1st impression
(London: The Bodley Head, 1944), p. 576]

31. Humbert writes a paper entitled "The Proustian theme in a
letter from Keats to Benjamin Bailey." This must refer to Keats' letter
of 22 November, 1817, wherein he discusses the truth of Imagination. For example:

But as I was saying—the simple imaginative Mind may have its rewards
in the repetition of its own silent Working coming continually on the Spirit
with a fine Suddenness—to compare great things with small—have you
never by being Surprised with an old Melody—in a delicious place—by a
delicious voice, felt over again your very Speculations and Surmises at the
time it first operated on your Soul—do you not remember forming to yourself the singer's face more beautiful than it was possible and yet with the
elevation of the Moment you did not think so—even than you were
mounted on the Wings of Imagination so high—that the Prototype must
be here after—that delicious face you will see. [*The Letters of John Keats*,
ed. M. B. Forman (Oxford University Press, 1935), p. 68]

The Proustian theme comes from Chapter III of *Le Temps Retrouvé*,
where Marcel develops the idea of an identical sensory perception
uniting the present moment and the past, and sees how imagination
frees him from the bondage of time. The Keatsian theme of possible
endless repetition in the imagination with increased pleasure is
paralleled. No brief quote can adequately convey Proust's ideas. See
The Past Recaptured, trans. F. Blossom (New York: Modern Library, n.d.), p. 191 ff.

32. Playing his final scene cheerfully, Cue says: "You recall Kipling: *Une femme est une femme, mais un caporal est une cigarette.*"
His version of "A woman is only a woman, but a good cigar is a
smoke." (See Kipling's "The Betrothed.")

33. Apropos of his Arctic expedition, our hero mentions "a
weather station on Pierre Point in Melville Sound." This is an allusion
to Melville's melodramatic *Pierre; or, the Ambiguities.*

34. Humbert uses two French phrases which he says are from Ronsard: *adolori d'amoureuse langueur* and *la vermeillette fente*. It may be that Hum added *adolori* (a pun on Lolita's real name) himself. This is the closest I can come in Ronsard's *Amours:*

> Postes des amoureux, va conter ma langueur . . .
>
> [Sonets pour Helen, Livre II, XXIX]
>
> Phare amoureux, qui guide ma langueur . . .
>
> [Livre des Amours, XLVII]
>
> Un diverse amoureuse langueur . . .
>
> [CLII]
>
> Autant que moy d'amoureuse langueur . . .
>
> [CCVI]

At first I was unable to uncover the source of *la vermeillette fente* (which Humbert quotes on page 49), finding that Ronsard usually blushes *despuis le nombril, jusqu'aux fesses,* as in *Élégie à Janet* where, after describing a lovely belly-button, he asks:

> Qu'attend tu plus? portray moy l'autre chose
> Qui est si belle, et que dire je n'ose.

But in one rarely printed sonnet he does *ose:*

> Je te salue, ô vermeillette fente,
> Qui, vivement, entre ces flancs reluis;
> Je te salue, ô bien heuré pertuis
> Qui rens me vie heureusement contente.
>
> C'est toy qui fais que plus ne me tourmente
> L'Archer vollant qui cause mes ennuis:
> T'aiant tenu seulement quatre nuits,
> Je sens sa force en moi desja plus lente.
>
> O petit trou, trou mignard, trou velu,
> D'un poil folet mollement crepelu,
> Qui à ton gré domptes les plus rebelles:
>
> Tous vers galans devroient pour t'honorer,
> A deux genoux te venir adorer,
> Tenant au poin leurs flambantes chandelles.
>
> [L'Enfer des Classiques, pp. 45–46]

35. The Goethe-Scott allusion comes when Humbert tells of taking Lolita to the Elphinstone hospital: "With a heterosexual Erlkönig in pursuit, thither I drove, half-blinded by the royal sunset . . ." (p. 242). This is a play on "The Erl-King," Scott's version of Goethe's ballad. It begins:

> O, who rides by night thro' the woodland so wild?
> It is the fond father embracing his child . . .

The Erl-King says to the child (the father can't hear):

> "O come and go with me, thou loveliest child;
> By many a gay sport shall thy time be beguiled . . .

Of course, in the ballad the child is a boy—Humbert has a suspicious tendency to call others homosexual, and this is how he interprets the poem and why he says a heterosexual elf king (Quilty) pursues him. In the poem the Erlkönig's deathly chill takes the child (as the chill wind takes Annabel Lee). An alarming association for Humbert.

Though Charles Kinbote expresses his admiration for Goethe's poem (*Pale Fire*, Commentary, line 662), and translates part of it into Zemblan, and though Nabokov has called the German "hallucinatory" (*Eugene Onegin*, Commentary, II, 235), I think Humbert has Scott's version in mind, because its beguiling lilt fits Lolita better than the gutteral German (how could *Knabe* ever suggest Lolita). —The relative rarity of allusions to German literature shows Humbert's culture is primarily French and English.

36. This has got to be sheer chance, but I will mention it anyway: Lo tells Hum that Quilty was a sexual freak who arranged sundry disgusting orgies, that he "just could not imagine . . . what they all did at Duk Duk Ranch." Earlier she says the dude ranch has "some silly name—Duk Duk Ranch—*you* know, just plain silly." I suspect this is some kind of clue or allusion for the reader, but as it happens there is, in New Pomerania, a primitive society called the Duk Duks; it is known particularly for its secret societies with various bizarre ceremonies and ordeals of initiation (which are not, however, sexual in nature).

37. It probably dates 1270-75. And there is an anonymous fragment, *Berthe de li gran pié*, which is some seventy years older. See

Arthur Sideleau, *Chansons de Geste* (Montréal: Thérien Frères Limitée, 1945), pp. 14-33.

38. There is something similar in *Pnin*. A couple's dog is named Sobakevich: this means "dog" (or "son of a dog," "MacDog") in Russian and is the name of one of the main characters in Gogol's *Dead Souls*. But the couple knows no Russian. —Incidentally, although Nabokov denies the influence, Gogol's grotesqueries occasionally come to mind when reading Nabokov. There are many allusions to Gogol in his works, some obvious (as in *The Gift* or *Pnin*), some less obvious (as in *The Eye* when the narrator's dream ends, "yes, yes, this sometimes happens to girls . . . A very rare phenomenon, but it happens"—a line from Gogol's "Nose"). But there are few direct borrowings, like these from "The Carriage" and *Dead Souls:*

The footmen, recruited from among the town's most adroit dandies—the best representatives of its purple youth—briskly served the food (sometimes even leaping across the table with a dish) . . . [*Invitation to a Beheading*, pp. 182-183]

His mother blew her nose with an extraordinarily loud trumpet sound. [*Invitation to a Beheading*, p. 134]

Pratt . . . rubbed her index finger under her nostrils with such vigor that her nose performed a kind of war dance. [*Lolita*, p. 199]

It is amazing how many writers have visited the Promontory of Noses.

39. *Madame Bovary*, trans. Joan Charles (Garden City: International Collectors Library, n.d.), p. 226.

40. After this the poetry turns to pus, blood, and ghastly screeching as Baudelaire indulges his macabre and stupid bad taste.

41. The poem itself is among the most asinine in print—full of "fierce fingers," stings and snakes, bruising kisses, bosom-biting and cadavers. The few good alliterations are flooded in blood.

42. On the Lolita-rose theme, see below, page 118.

43. Later Quilty conjectures Dolores may have made phone calls to "Paradise, Wash., Hell Canyon."

44. He mentions the poem briefly ("dreadful") in the Notes on Prosody in his Commentary on *Onegin*, III, 523.

45. Excepting a very minor character in a thing called *Huasi-pungo* by one Jorge Icaza.

46. H. -R. Lenormand, *Théâtre Complet* (Paris, 1942), X, 181. Original spelling used.

47. Other things about Humbert Humbert suggest Chichikovian *poshlost'*—the purple robe and silk pajamas he is so proud of, the perfumes he douses his middle-aged flesh with, and his extreme fastidiousness, all find parallels in *Dead Souls*.

48. Ovid, *The Art of Love*, trans. R. Humphries (Bloomington, Ind., 1958).

49. Verlaine's second "Nevermore" also contains lines which are appropriate at this point and may be at periscope depth in Humbert's mind:

> Le Bonheur a marché côté à côté avec moi,
> Mais la FATALITÉ ne connaît point de trêve:
> Le vers est dans le fruit, le réveil dans le rêve,
> Et le remords est dans l'amour: telle est la loi.

50. The references to "Annabel Lee" were first noted (but not listed or satisfactorily interpreted) by Lionel Trilling, "The Last Lover—Nabokov's *Lolita*," *Encounter*, XI, 4 (1959), pp. 9–19.

51. And, Nabokov the artist would probably add, meaningless and ridiculous.

52. The italics in this line and in all quotations which follow are my own unless otherwise specified.

53. The name of Humbert's father's seaside hotel where little Hum met Annabel Leigh.

54. Compare Humbert's rationalizations to Sade's:

"Here is Virgil who could the nymphet sing in single tone . . . Here are two of King Akhnaten's and Queen Nefertiti's prenubile Nile daughters . . . wearing nothing but many necklaces . . . Here are some brides of ten compelled to seat themselves on the fascinum, the virile ivory in the temples of classical scholarship. Marriage and cohabitation before the age of puberty are still not uncommon in certain East-Indian provinces. Lepcha old men of eighty copulate with girls of eight, and nobody minds." [Part I, Chapter 5]

"The laws of Lycurgus, the model lawgiver, not only allowed fathers full rights over their children, but even condemned to death those whom the parents did not wish to raise or who were deformed . . . Almost all the women of Asia, Africa, and America cause themselves to miscarry without incurring disapproval; Cook encountered this custom in all the islands of the South Seas. Romulus permitted infanticide; the law of twelve tables allowed it as well. . . . Aristotle advocates this so-called crime . . ." [*Justine, or, The Misfortunes of Virtue*, trans. H. Weaver (New York, 1966), p. 101]

Justine is alluded to elsewhere in *Lolita*, and there may be other parallels, but the book is too vile for me to read through.

55. See Arthur Quinn, *E. A. Poe* (New York, 1941), p. 252. Perhaps not accidentally, Virginia Poe (alias Annabel Lee) died in 1847 —exactly 100 years before Humbert meets Lolita.

56. Actually it was Petersburg, Virginia. I suspect an attempt to avoid having Virginia in Virginia, or some private joke, rather than weak scholarship on Nabokov's part.

57. Like a magician Nabokov performs his tricks while focussing the readers' attention in the wrong place—nothing in Nabokov's stories is "for the heck of it."

58. Here we have a case of double association. "Lenore" and "my bird" suggest Poe, but one other phrase is taken from August Bürger's oft-translated ballad, *Lenore*. The last four lines of stanza twenty-three are:

> Und immer weiter, hop! hop! hop!
> Gings fort im sausende Galopp,
> Das Ross und Reiter schnoben,
> Und Kies und Junken stoben.

Bürger's ballad, like Poe's poem, echoes the theme of maidenly death.

59. Lolita dies on December 25, 1952. Annabel Leigh dies in December, 1923.

60. In *Speak, Memory* Nabokov's imagined lost teenage love is associated with Lenore:

It seems hardly worth while to add that, as themes go, my elegy dealt with the loss of a beloved mistress—Delia, Tamara or Lenore—whom I had never lost . . . [V. Nabokov, *Speak, Memory* (New York: Grosset & Dunlap, 1951), p. 163]

61. As Lionel Trilling notes "nymph" means "bride" in Greek.

62. Later in *Lolita* Humbert exclaims: "*finis*, my friends, *finis*, my fiends" (p. 271).

63. Describing how he wrote "The Raven" in "The Philosophy of Composition" Poe declared "the death of a beautiful woman is unquestionably the most poetical topic in the world." He used the theme in "A Paean" (an early version of "Annabel Lee") and "Ulalume" (written after Virginia Poe's death).

64. Humbert's first Annabel dies—very unpoetically—at age thirteen, a few months after he meets her.

65. Of course, it is true that Annabel was taken by the envious angels, as was Beatrice. But Humbert is insane, and he could very well attribute his own deed to the forces of fate.

66. And in one of those "accidents" of fate it turns out he would have been seen by Jean Farlow, that by not committing murder he had let fate go on inexorably, and Nabokovianly, to the point where all would work to his own advantage.

67. More direct allusions to Bluebeard are discussed below, p. 48.

68. I confess that I find Humbert at least as charming as he is sick.

69. Of course, there is a relationship between the two. He is a poet and a madman, a lover and a monster. He says:

The gentle and dreamy regions through which I crept were the patrimonies of poets . . .

Emphatically, no killers are we. Poets never kill.

A poet *à mes heures,* I composed a madrigal to the soot-black lashes of her pale-grey vacant eyes . . .

Several of his poetic efforts are given in the memoir: the maniac's masterpiece written after losing Lo, the poem he forces Quilty to read before killing him, a few lines of a "French ballad" sung to Rita, some nonsense verse for Lolita.

Simultaneously, he sees Lo as beauty, himself as beast *(ce monstre délicat)*. He has an "ape-ear" and an "ape-eye." Lo is his prey; he is a rattlesnake, a tiger, a spider, "nature's faithful hound," a "pentapod monster."

70. See below, Chapter III.

71. Apropos Poe wrote: "The *vagueness* of exaltation aroused by a sweet air (which should be strictly indefinite and never too strongly suggestive) is precisely what we should aim at in poetry." (Quinn, p. 429.)

72. On the other hand, prudish Humbert would probably snort that at least he wasn't a necrophiliac. All of which goes to show that one man's perversion is another man's pride.

73. Containing, perhaps, allusion to mythology—Poseidon (and one of his three brothers) or Nereus, one of several "old men of the sea." Later Humbert recalls:

Those ribald sea monsters. *"Mais allez-y, allez-y!"* Annabel skipping on one foot to get into her shorts, I seasick with rage, trying to screen her. [p. 55]

74. In *The Defense* the hero's recognition of these recurrent patterns in his life combines with his chess mania and his efforts to avoid the patterns and leads to his suicide.

75. See below, pp. 75–76, on the Charlotte-Lolita parallels.

76. When Humbert first sees Lo he says: "There was my Riviera love peering at me over dark glasses," and he feels like a king who has discovered a lost "princess"—no doubt in a kingdom or princedom by the sea.

77. Idle curiosity prompts me, but I think it would be interesting to know whether Nabokov originally conceived the Lolita-Annabel parallels as a conscious parody of Freudian theory or (what seems far more likely) whether he first used the allusions and the theme of repetition in man's life, only then deciding he had to poke fun at Freud so that readers would not draw erroneous conclusions about Humbert's conscious or unconscious acts, or Nabokov-Humbert's very conscious art.

78. Humbert does not provide the dates in his reconstructed journal, but by piecing together the bits of information scattered

through the memoir and consulting a perpetual calendar, the exact dates can be deduced. In fact, with a little Pninian research it is possible to construct a fairly exact calendar of all the events in the novel, including Lolita's birth on January 1, her liberation from Humbert on July 4, and her death on Christmas Day.

79. Dwarf Conductors = little car men.

80. Nabokov used the "something" device in an earlier work: "Closed shutters, a lighted candle, Gentle Jesus, meek and mild, something-something little child . . ." *Speak, Memory*, p. 51.

81. Carmencita = Little Carmen = Dwarf Conductors—a complicated bilingual pun.

82. *Les Contes de Perrault* (Paris: Alphonse Lemerre, 1880), p. 132.

83. This may also be an allusion to "the old man of the sea and his brother" who ribaldly interrupt Humbert when he is nervously trying to make Annabel Leigh on the beach of the Riviera—many years before meeting Lolita.

84. Prosper Merimée, *Carmen* (Paris: Ernest Flammarion, n.d.), p. 69.

85. Merimée corresponded with Pushkin's friend Sergei Sobolevsky. He was full of admiration for Pushkin's works, and later (1849–52) he worked on translations of *The Queen of Spades* and *The Gypsies*. See L. Kogan, "Pushkin v perevodax Merimée," *Vremennik puškinskoj komissii*, 4–5 (Moscow-Leningrad, 1939), pp. 331–56. Also H. Mongault, "Pouchkine en France," *Revue de Littérature comparée*, No. 17 (1937), and B. Tomaševskij, *Puškin i Francija* (Leningrad, 1960).

Pushkin had a high opinion of Merimée too. His *Songs of the Western Slavs* are for the most part verse versions of Merimée's *La Guzla*, a literary fake which fooled Pushkin.

86. The story is usually interpreted as Pushkin's debunking of the Byronic hero. But Pushkin's attitude toward his characters is seldom that simple. Surely he felt some sympathy for Aleko; after all, Zemfira *is* a bitch.

87. This is one of several words which are phonetic, anagrammatic disguises of *Quilty*'s name: *Quel*quepar*t* Island.

88. On the other hand it is true that the words to the song alone (pp. 63–64) should be enough to create some false expectation.

CHAPTER II

1. A well-intentioned *double entendre* which in not very polite Parisian circles translates as: "Get up, prick, it's time to die." —Of course, "to die" means to have an orgasm.

2. The triple repetition is a mark of Quilty's style—recall the parody of Shakespeare: "to borrow and to borrow and to borrow."

3. *Qui*pped—one of a number of purely phonetic clues.

4. The soft drink pun is repeated later.

5. He probably did since Quilty has been following them.

6. And at the end of Chapter 20, Part I, Jean Farlow says of Ivor: "Last time he told me a completely indecent story about his nephew. It appears—"

7. In a typically Nabokovian reversal (worst fears being realized) she will "remind" Humbert and laugh.

8. When Lo pointed out Quilty to Humbert at The Enchanted Hunters, Quilty was wearing "loud checks" (p. 123).

9. Humbert advises us that the play "has overtones of Maeterlinck, Lenormand and various quiet British dreamers." Enchanted forests teeming with blue birds and futuristic fairies are part of Maeterlinck's dreary stock-in-trade. I began a search for some specific work that would contain direct parallels, but soon decided there are some sacrifices even scholars should have sense enough not to make. I did come across a work by Lenormand containing what seem to be echoes of Quilty's *The Hunted Enchanters*. In *La Folle du Ciel* (Féerix en deux partis, 1937), the main characters are: The Hunter, The Fowler, The Hunter's Mother, and The Gull. In a Norwegian forest The Gull falls in love with The Hunter, and aided by a friendly neighborhood Troll, is transformed from gull into girl. The Hunter is delighted, and a child soon results from their union. After a lover's quarrel, the girl wishes herself back into the aviary, seemingly a tragic end to a woodland tale. But there are more complications, interspersed with idiotic conversations between auks and parakeets, and squacking dialogue like this:

LA MOUETTE

Toi . . . toi . . .

LA CHASSEUR

Moi.

LA MOUETTE

Moi.

LA CHASSEUR

Toi. Moi . . . Toi.

LA MOUETTE

Pas tuer moi.

LA CHASSEUR

Non. Jamais.

LA MOUETTE

Toi, homme. Moi, femme.

Which is vaguely reminiscent of a Tarzan movie. But in a general way some motifs do suggest Quilty's opuscule owes this play a debt. See H. -R. Lenormand, *Théâtre Complet* (Paris, 1938), Volume 9.

10. Gaston-Gustave thinks the open queen may be a "trap."

11. This "perhaps" is a piece of camouflage.

12. Nabokov constantly taunts his readers by assuring them what a simple task it is to figure things out.

13. Another clue is in the Chestnut Motel-Kasbeam section. See above, p. 18.

14. Concerning Humbert's style, note the complex irregularity of the sequence of tenses in this sentence—the sudden ambiguous (and grammatically "impossible") shift from the past tense of a memoir to the present tense of an interior monologue.

15. Earlier his name was Mr. Swine.

16. A fleeting geographical clue comprehensible only to Michiganders is Humbert's note that one of his quarrels with Lo was: "On McEwen St., corner of Wheaton Ave., in a Michigan town bearing his name" (p. 161). "His" is Quilty's. There is in fact a town named Clare in Michigan.

17. Stephen Crane's "The Blue Hotel"?

18. Perhaps an allusion to the heroine of Goethe's *The Sorrows of Young Werther*.

19. Quilty himself says, "I have made private movies out of *Justine* and other eighteenth-century sexcapades" (p. 300).

CHAPTER III

1. ". . . I had to abandon my natural idiom, my untrammeled, rich, and infinitely docile Russian tongue for a second-rate brand of English . . ." "On a Book Entitled *Lolita*."

2. Let me immediately confess I am not bilingual. Still, no one whose tastes have been formed by Pushkin, Lermontov, and Tolstoy can find Nabokov's Russian style exemplary, even where (*Otchajanie*, for example) it is less complex than in *Dar*. "Ornamental prose" was among the interesting but unfortunate fads in Russian literature of the 1920's and 1930's.

3. Among the writers who have influenced Nabokov (no matter how testily he denies it) are Gogol and Bely, both of whom were exponents and practitioners of prose-poetry.

4. I find "a mobile Adam's apple" in *Speak, Memory*, p. 36.

5. In *The Gift* he used an analogous Russian alliteration: *szadi nee zamedlennymi zigzagami. Dar* (New York, 1952), p. 39.

6. Phonetically analogous to "blue and bronze-colored blobs." *Speak, Memory*, p. 34.

7. If we go back a few decades to the Russian of *Dar*, we find that in general Nabokov was noticeably less concerned with instrumentation; but the repetition of whole syllables is used with some regularity: *pegas peg, tom tomnyx, malen'kij malajskij, lampada lamy, gorodit' ogorod, bazar na zare, ražij graždanin, probuja i aprobiruja.*

8. I think I should offer some proof that Humbert's style is the same as Nabokov's. Here are a number of examples of various kinds of sound play in *Speak, Memory;* these show how close it is to the style of *Lolita*. First, alphabetically, some fairly simple examples of alliteration and assonance:

adventurous ancestors, abnormal aptitude, bracken and bindweed, beribboned and beflowered; benches, bridges and boles; broken brown blossoms, creaked and crackled, dismally drag, dreaded remnants of delirium's dilating world, Frenchlessly and unflinchingly, gouache and guano, gluey glistening (bland bent, slight slant), heart-broken hiccough, interruptions and innovations, the immortal and the immature, lolling and loafing, unravel the labyrinthine frets on the linoleum, from Maikov to Maiakovsky, the mysterious of mimicry, mild myopic eyes, noseless and noiseless, pallid poetry, paradisiac personages, primly pessimistic, to poke and peer, to penetrate my penumbral covert, pleasant pyrrhic acceleration, papery pepper-and-salt bark, rigid religion, simple symmetry, smiling similes, summer *soomerki*, slow-motioned slouch, slight slant, tremulous trail, torpid trot, vividly visualized

Some more sophisticated couplings:

ancient escutcheon, brittle umbrella, blood-colored alcohol, dapper captors, grizzled muzzle, irrelevant recollection, multiple manipulations, palpable people, recapitulatory implications, reticulated tenderness, stickily glistening, bespoke a speck, vesperal suspense

And some longer sequences:

a lone light dimly diluted the darkness

delicately pluck and proffer a leaf

in its nimbus the mist seemed transformed into a visible drizzle

among mountain snows, or a mauve remoteness melting beyond moving masts

sitting as stiffly as if he were stuffed

somewhat somnambulistic ascension in self-engendered darkness

A few minor rhymes:

the epitaphical simile unwittingly echoes, I note, an epigraphical theme

skim rapidly along the rim

tip, leaf, dip, relief—

Of course every writer uses some alliteration, but I think the Nabokov stamp is clearly on these examples as it is on the ones from Lolita. In revising translations of his Russian novels he often sacrifices strict literalness to euphony. Thus in *The Gift, snisxoditel'nyj otbor* becomes "lenient eliminations" (p. 85).

9. "Every limb of every limpid letter . . ." (*Speak, Memory*, p. 66).

10. It has already been shown that writers can be identified, after some study, by the percentage of words beginning with different letters of the alphabet which occurs in a sufficient sample. See George U. Yule, *Statistical Study of Literary Vocabulary* (Cambridge, 1944).

11. While I wouldn't want to insult Nabokov, there are some minor similarities between Johnson's style and his—including the frequent use of syntactical pairs and a predilection for musty items from lexical limbo. See the first three chapters of W. K. Wimsatt, *The Prose Style of Samuel Johnson* (New Haven: Yale University Press, 1963).

12. See A. A. Saburov, "*Vojna i mir*" *L. N. Tolstogo* (Moscow, 1959) and R. F. Christian, *Tolstoy's 'War and Peace': A Study* (Oxford, 1962).

13. Also: "John had to see a customer and
Jean had to feed her dogs."

14. As further proof that Humbert's style is Nabokov's style, here are a few doublets from *Speak, Memory*: "Near a white garden bench, on a round garden table"; "falsely clear or falsely recondite"; "all forms of vitality are forms of velocity"; "combining rhythmic pattern with rhythmic sound"; "gamblers kept steadily playing for steadily sparkling stakes"; "the little black dog with very white teeth"; "The sweet-tempered sire of a ferocious family"; "a lacquered box with licorice sticks"; "Camberwell Beauties with creamy borders"; "pathetic ladies' posthumous love"; "I pursued rose-margined Sulphurs, grey-marbled Satyrs"; "The old and the new"; "the liberal touch and the patriarchal one"; "fatal poverty and fatalistic wealth."

15. A concolorous example from Pope:

> Not louder shrieks to pitying heaven are cast,
> When husbands, or when lap dogs breathe their last.

16. Other examples: "*in an*gry *in*audible speech"; "her *autob*iography was as devoid of interest as her *autop*sy would have been"; "Jean, with her always *trembl*ing fingers, took me by the *temples*,

and, tears in her bright blue eyes, attempted, unsuccessfully, to glue herself to my lips."

17. Related, no doubt, to Dr. Rosetta Stone in *Pnin*.

18. Humbert suffers from *"pavor nocturnus"* during childhood.

19. Perhaps an allusion to O'Neill's *Desire Under the Elms* or to Berlin's *Unter den Linden*.

20. The suffix -ward is one of Humbert's favorites: streetward, cupward, lobby-ward, campward.

Incidentally, another feature by which Humbert-Nabokov's style may be identified is the metaphor on "wake," as in: (paper whirling) "in the wake of the observation car"; "Humbert lumbering in her [Monique's] narrow wake"; "to the west of my wake"; (going through the market) "in the wake of Professor W."; (nurse) "rushed after me so as to be able to slam the door in my wake"; "I myself followed him . . . bouncing up twice in his wake."

21. See George Puttenham, *The Arte of English Poesie* (Cambridge, 1936).

22. Compare: "dashing across the palpitating *plage*," *Speak, Memory*, p. 99.

23. Of course it was ridiculous of me to expect he would perform clever tricks like a trained seal.

24. Compare these snapping shadow effects from two other works:

. . . when a man who had been dozing on a bench beneath a bright whitewashed wall at last got up to help me find my way, his blue shadow on the wall did not immediately follow him. [*Invitation to a Beheading*, p. 52]

For one moment, thanks to the sudden radiance of a lone lamp where the station square ends, a grossly exaggerated shadow, also holding a muff, races beside the sleigh, climbs a billow of snow, and is gone. [*Speak, Memory*, p. 61]

25. As I have already said, *Speak, Memory* is very closely related to *Lolita* in many ways—style, specific phrases, certain characters, allusions, and imagery. Though one should not draw any ridiculous conclusions from it (that she played the role of a Louise Colet, for example), the fact is that parts of the Annabel Leigh section of *Lolita* are paralleled by the Colette episode in *Speak, Memory*

(Chapter 7). Little Nabokov meets a ten-year-old girl on the Riviera beach and falls in (obviously non-sexual) love:

. . . when I met Colette, I knew at once this was the real thing. Colette seemed to me so much stranger than all my other chance playmates at Biarritz! [p. 101]

The name *Colette* is concolorous with *Lolita*, and the imagery of the Colette section is almost exactly like the imagery in *Lolita*. We see Colette: ". . . tap-tapping her glinting hoop through sun and shade" (p. 103). Then:

. . . she runs with her hoop ever faster around me and finally dissolves among the slender shadows cast on the graveled path by the interlaced arches of its low looped fence. [p. 104]

Humbert wants to take Lolita-Carmen to Mexico. Compare this to what Nabokov says of Colette:

Where did I want to take her? Spain? America? The mountains above Pau? *"La-bas, la-bas, dans la montagne,"* as I heard Carmen sing at the opera. [p. 102]

The sun-shade imagery is used repeatedly in *Speak, Memory* as in *Lolita;* not surprisingly—but characteristically—it is often connected to the theme of memory:

Judging by the strong sunlight that, when I think of this revelation, immediately invades my memory with lobed sun flecks through overlapping patterns of greenery . . . [p. 3]

I see the tablecloth and the faces of seated people sharing in the animation of light and shade beneath a moving, a fabulous foliage, exaggerated, no doubt, by the same faculty of impassioned commemoration . . . [p. 122]

. . . the eye of memory is so firmly focussed upon a small figure squatting on the ground . . . that the various loci—Berlin, Prague, Franzensbad, Paris, the Riviera, Paris again, Cap d'Antibes and so forth—lose all their sovereignty, pool their petrified generals and fallen leaves, cement the friendship of their interlocked paths, and unite in a federation of light and shade . . . [p. 235]

With one blow, the room would be cleft into light and shade. The foliage of the birches moving in the sun had the translucent green tone of grapes . . . [p. 79]

. . . I remember the dreamy flow of punts and canoes on the Cam, the Hawaiian whine of phonographs slowly passing through sunshine and shade . . . [p. 200]

The sun and shade imagery occurs in most of his other novels too, but not so insistently. I find Mrs. Luzhin "passing alternately through sunlight and shadow" (p. 55). See also *The Defense*, p. 159, p. 166; *Invitation to a Beheading*, p. 51, p. 121; *Pnin*, p. 17, p. 129. And "A linden where light and shadow mingle," *Eugene Onegin*, Commentary, III, 523.

Another *Lolita-Speak, Memory* parallel is the allusion to Poe in recalling the loss of a teen-age love:

. . . my elegy dealt with the loss of a beloved mistress—Delia, Tamara or Lenore—whom I had never lost, never loved, never met but was all set to meet, love, lose. [p. 163]

One can find themes and characters from *Lolita* adumbrated in several other early works. The parallels between *Lolita* and *Laughter in the Dark* are particularly striking. Margot, the bitchy, tennis-playing, sixteen year-old heroine of that novel, is one of *Lolita's* closest relatives—one might suspect that Harold Haze, or Charlotte Becker, had visited Berlin. Compare, for example, the *"enfin seuls"* of *Lolita* (Part I, Chapter 27) to that of *Laughter* (Chapter 18), and, especially, the "nowhere" of *Laughter* (end of Chapter 21) to that of *Lolita* (end of Part I).

26. In *Speak, Memory:* "a dank, dark, satisfying blend of damp moss" (p. 23).

27. *Speak, Memory*, p. 84. Cryptograms play a minor role in this deception. In *Speak, Memory* (p. 38) Nabokov tells us his Uncle Ruka "turned the sequence '5.13 24.11 13.16 9.13.5 5.13 24.11' into the opening words of a famous monolog in Shakespeare." He leaves it to the reader to discover that $5 = T$, $9 = N$, $11 = E$, $13 = O$, $16 = R$, and $24 = B$.

28. See, for example, Godunov-Cherdyntsev's conversation with himself at the end of Chapter One of *The Gift*.

29. Compare a color and memory passage from *The Defense:*

. . . and with this snowy recollection there would float up once more against a background of night the celebrated writer's villa . . . and the cleared path and snowdrifts illumined by electric light, phantasmal stripes on the dark snow. These men with their various occupations, each of whom tinted her recollection his own particular color . . . [p. 88]

30. There are dozens of examples in the works I have read. They suggest a peculiar way of perceiving the world and an artistic sensibility to forms, colors, and textures akin to that of Proust or Rilke. See Appendix A for a list of examples.

31. "Lo" and "purse" are puns.

32. The toad is Nabokov's favorite simile amphibian. In *The Gift: s . . . poxožim na žabu bul'dogom* ("with . . . a bulldog resembling a toad"). In the Commentary to *Onegin,* "That sheep look like toads and can devastate a continent did not concern poets" (Volume II, p. 322).

33. Compare this to the following sad triple metaphor from *Pnin:*

. . . young émigré poets, who had left Russia in their pale, unpampered pubescence, chanted nostalgic elegies dedicated to a country that could be little more to them than a sad stylized toy, a bauble found in the attic, a crystal globe which you shake to make a soft luminous snowstorm inside over a minuscule fir tree and a log cabin of papier maché. [*Pnin* (New York: Atheneum, 1965), pp. 44–45]

34. See, for example, p. 129.

35. And sometimes he is intentionally playful, as in: "Let me tell you, however, something" (p. 94).

APPENDIX B

1. Here I am inclined to suspect a slip-up on Nabokov's part. The brother dies at four when Lolita is two, and she was conceived on a "honeymoon trip" to Vera Cruz. Though Charlotte likes her bed, it is hard to imagine prim Mrs. Haze, a woman of most honorable principles, having an illegitimate child and talking about him all the time.

2. These dates are calculated (with the aid of a perpetual calendar) on the basis of the stated time of Humbert's arrival in Ramsdale and the sequence of days listed in his diary.

3. According to the information provided, this has to be the proper date and day, but July 29 did not fall on a Sunday in 1947. See footnote 5 below.

4. Humbert's calendar is not even internally consistent. He says his cohabitation with Charlotte lasted fifty days, but he couldn't have married her before June 25 (given state laws, probably not before the 28th), and she dies only forty-four days after that.

5. The 15th was not a Wednesday that year. What throws things off is probably Humbert's bad memory—he notes it was "around August 15" when he picked up Lolita at Camp Q. He also states it was Wednesday. I have to accept his word, so here the dates from July 29 to August 24 are given according to the Humbertian calendar rather than the Gregorian one. This is a good example of relativity in fiction. (A fellow Russian scholar has noted that *Anna Karenina* begins on both a Thursday and a Friday.)

6. Humbert includes the postmark as documentation.

7. Another example of Humbert's messy time-keeping. He mentions spending fifty-six days in the asylum and in jail writing his memoir. But there are not fifty-six days between September 25 (the day of his arrest) and November 16 (the day of his death).

INDEX

This index has been so compiled that the reader can easily check any name, allusion, clue, or device that he may be interested in. Among the items included are: titles and names of characters and places used in *Lolita*; titles, names of characters, and authors to whom there are allusions; specific stylistic devices; topics taken up in the novel and in *Keys to* Lolita. The Calendar is not indexed. Italicized page numbers refer to the Notes.

Adam and Eve, 10

Alcott, Louisa, 21

Aleko. *See* Pushkin, *The Gypsies*

Alliteration: examples, 82–97, 102–103, *147–149;* rondo, 85–87; voiced-unvoiced pairs, 88; liquids, 88–89; nasals, 88; parallelism in doublets, 90–92; invention of children, 93; use in ads, 92–93

Allusion: contextual, 18, 23–26, 31–52; to Russian literature, 20–21; English literature, 19–20; French literature, 21; list of authors, 21–23; purpose of, 37–40; deceptive, 50–53. *See also* individual authors and titles

Andersen, Hans Christian, *134*

"Annabel Lee." *See* Poe

Annabel Leigh, 9–10, 29, 34–35, 41–45, 76, 118, *142–144, 150–151.* See also "Annabel Lee"; Joyce

Aristophanes, 15

Assonance, 86–97, 102–103, *147–148*

Aztec Red, 18, 78, 108, 128, 129

Balmont, Konstantin, 82

Baudelaire, Charles, 26, 28, *139*

Beale, Fred, 6

Beardsley, Aubrey, 16

Belleau, Remy, *134–135*

Belloc, Hilaire, 20

Bely, Andrey, 97, 101, *147*

Berthe, 24, *138–139*

Blake, William, 27–28

Bluebeard. *See* Perrault

Briceland Gazette, 60, 77

Broughton, Hugh, 27

Browning, Robert: "Soliloquy of a Spanish Cloister," 16–17; "Pippa Passes," 20, 26, *133*

Bryusov, Valery, 21

Bumper, Harry. *See* Sheridan

Bürger, August, *135, 141*

Burke, Barbara, 6, 7

Butterflies, 4, 13

Byrd, Avis, 96

Calendar: general time references, 125–130, *131, 141, 143–144, 153–154;* Independ-

Calendar—*continued*
  ence Day, 7, 57; summer equi-
  nox, 46; Christmas, 53
Carroll, Lewis, 22
Catullus, 22
Cavall, 24
Cervantes, 17
Champion, Colorado, 67, 72
Chateaubriand, René, 4, 101,
  131
Chekov, Anton, 20, 30, 89
Chess, 5, 8, 110, 112
Chestnut Lodge, 18, *146*
Chimène. *See* Corneille
Christie, Agatha, 57
Chum, 47, 50, 63
Cicero, 89
Clare, Aunt, 73. *See* Quilty,
  Clare
Clare, Michigan, *146*
Clues, phonetic. *See* Query, Qui-
  etly, Quim, Quimby, Quipped,
  Quix
Cocteau, Jean, 22
Coleridge, Samuel, 12–13
Conrad, Joseph, 81
Conrad, Udo, *Laughter in the
  Dark*, 81
Corneille, *Le Cid*, 71–72
Crane, Stephen, *147*

Dahl, Mona, 25, 65–66, 70–71,
  133
Dante, 26–27, 37, *142*
Dark Age, 58, 60, 61
Darkbloom, Vivian, 11, 58, 61–
  62, 96
Defense, The, 5, *143*, *152–153*

Delalande, Pierre, 3, *131*
Despair (Otchajanie), *146*
Dialogue, 114–115
"Dolores." *See* Swinburne
Dostoevsky, 3, 4, 20
Double entendre, 57, 65, 66, 96,
  99, *145*, *153*
Doublets, 89–93, *149*
Doyle, Arthur Conan, 96
Dromes, 63–64
Duk Duk, *138*

Elphinstone, 7, 47, *138*
Emperor, Miss. *See* Flaubert
Enchanted Hunters, The, 18, 32,
  33, 60, 63, 64–69, 72–74, 77,
  96, 118, *145*. *See Hunted En-
  chanters, The*
Eryx, 14, 15, 96
Eye, The, *139*

Fantazia (Fantasia), Stella, 8,
  132
Farlow, John and Jean, 24
Flaubert, Gustave: *Madame Bovary*, 24–26, 67–68, 85; *Éducation Sentimentale*, 135
Freud, Sigmund, 13, 14, 15, 43–
  45, *143*

Galsworthy, John, 22
Gershenzon, M. O., 70
Gide, André, 22
Gift, The (Dar), 2, 20, 81, 101,
  131, *139*, *147*, *149*, *152*, *153*
Godin, Gaston, 67–68, 112, 118
Goethe, Wolfgang, 22, *138*, *147*
Gogol, Nikolai, 21, 31, 78, 89,
  97, 101, *132*, *139*, *140*, *147*

Gold, Edusa, 65, 66, 69, 77, 96–97
Gold, Electra, 92, 96–97
Goldoni, Carlo, 12
Grimm Road, 96, 108

Haze, Charlotte, 6, 8, 23–24, 33, 37, 39, 75–76, 92, 102, 113, 115, 153, 154
Haze, Dolores. See Lolita
Hero of Our Time, A, 110, 118
Holmes, Charlie, 6–7, 130
Hopkins, Gerard Manley, 22
Hourglass Lake, 39, 74–76
Hugo, Victor, 22
Humbert Humbert: character of, 118, 142–143; his name, 8–9, 132
Hunted Enchanters, The, 57, 61, 65–71, 99, 145
Hunter, Ted, 18

Ibsen, Henrik, 22
Imagery: characteristics and examples, 105–114, 121–124, 148–151; photographic, 109–110; reflection, 111–112; sun and shade, 106–108, 148–151; water, 112
Instrumentation. See Alliteration, Assonance, Doublets
Invitation to a Beheading, 139, 152

Johnson, Samuel: The Rambler, 15; style of, 89, 149
Joyce, James: Finnegans Wake, 9–10, 132, 135–136; Portrait of an Artist, 10; Ulysses, 10–11, 20, 132; other allusions to, 9–11, 62, 97–98, 101

Kasbeam, 18, 67
Keats, John, 136
Kilmer, Joyce, 22
Kipling, Rudyard, 136
Kitzler, 14
Kreutzer Sonata, The. See Tolstoy

Lady Who Loved Lightning, The, 58, 61–62, 70
Laqueue, 57, 145
Larousse, Pierre, 12
Lancelot of the Lake, 132
Laughter in the Dark, 152
Leblanc, Maurice, 12, 57
Lenormand, Henri, 30–31, 145–146
Lester, Miss and Miss Fabian, 96
Lexicon, 99
Lindy. See Sopwith
Little Nymph, The, 58, 59, 65
Lizzarabengoa, José. See Merimée, Carmen
Lolita (Haze):
—Angelic antecedents, 26–27
—Demonic antecedents, 26–31
—Her name, 30, 59, 95, 98–99
—Humbert's love for, 40–42
—Other literary Lolitas, 30, 138
—Smile of, 18, 62, 66–67, 69
Lolita:
—Class-list, 8, 16
—Emotional tone of, 40–41
—Genesis of, 3–4

—Junk dog in, 6
—License plate numbers in, 18–19
—Motel registers, 11–18, *133*
—Names of characters, 9–10, 11–18, 24, 25, 47–48, 95–97
—"On a Book Entitled *Lolita*," 4, 7–8
—Opening lines of, 35–36, 104–105
—Satire in, 118–119
—Weather in, 108–109
Lore, Ann, 48–49
Lore, Mary, 47–49
Love under the Lindens, 99, *150*
Lucas. *See* Merimée, *Carmen*
Lupin, Arsène. *See* Leblanc, M.

Maeterlinck, Maurice, 13, 66, *145*
Marat, 23
Marlowe, Christopher, 31
Maturin, Charles, 30
MacCoo, Virginia, 10
McFate, Aubrey, 70
Melampus, 24
Melville, Herman, 89, *136*
Memory, 42–43, 74–76, 110–111
Merimée, Prosper: *Carmen*, 16, 26, 34, 39, 40, 45–52; and Pushkin, *144*
Merrymay, Pa. *See* Merimée, Prosper
Metaphors, 112–114, *150*
Milne, A. A., 20
Molière, 13, 96

Morell, James Mavor, 15
My Cue, 61. *See* Quilty, Clare

Nabokov, Vladimir: cleverness of, 78; his view of art, 109–110; Russian style compared to English, 81, *147*; television interview, 104; use of colors, 110
Names of characters. See *Lolita:* Names of characters
Navel, 130, *137*
Neologisms, 100–101
Nightmares. *See* Ovid

Orgon, D. *See* Molière
Ovid, 32

Pale Fire, 114, *133, 134, 138*
Pavor Manor, 96
Perrault, Charles, 40, 48
Persians, 60–61, 64
Petrarch, 27
Piano lessons. *See* Flaubert
Picador, Lucas. *See* Merimée
Pim. *See* Milne
Pippa. *See* Browning
Pnin, *139, 150, 152, 153*
Poe, Edgar, 33, *133–134, 141, 142, 143*
—"Annabel Lee," 26, 34–37, 39–41, 43, 59, 69, 105, *140*. *See* Annabel Leigh
—"Lenore," 37, 38, 39
—Parody of, 41–42
—"Raven, The," 33, 37–39
—Virginia Clem, 37, 39, 41
Poquelin, Jean, 23. *See* Molière
Porlock. *See* Coleridge

Proust, Marcel, 101, *136*

Puns, 98–99

Pushkin, Alexander, *144, 147*

—*Eugene Onegin* (and Commentary), 4, 20, 82, 94, 110–111, 114, *132, 135, 138, 139, 152, 153*

—"Gypsies, The," 21, 47–52

—*Mozart and Salieri,* 118

—"Queen of Spades, The," 68

—"Station Master, The," 70

Quelquepart Island, 16, 50, 73, *144*

Query, 74

Quietly, 75

Quick, 74

Quilty, Clare, 7, 11, 19f., 48f., 57–78, *132, 133, 145*

Quilty, Ivor, 62–63, 77, *145*

Quim, 14, 15, 73

Quimby, Phineas, 14, 73

Quine the Swine, 59, 72. *See* Quilty, Clare

Quix, 17, 73

Rahab. *See* Blake

Rainbow. *See* Rimbaud

Randall, Johnny, 15

Rhymes, 87–88, *148*

Rhythm, 101–105

Rimbaud, Arthur, 13

Rita, 73–74

Rolland, Romain, 23

Ronsard, Pierre, *136*

Roses, 60, 64, 117–118

Rostand, Edmond, 23

Rousseau, Jean-Jacques, 9, 23

Sade, Count de, 57, 77, *140–141, 147*

Sanchicha. *See* Browning

Schiller, Richard F., 50, 52, 96, 99

Schmetterling. *See* Maeterlinck; Butterfly

Schwarzmann, Blanche, 96

Scott, Walter, *138*

Shakespeare, 18–19, *133, 145*

Shaw, George Bernard, 15

Sheridan, Richard, 14, 96

Similes, 89, 113–114

Skiller, Dick. *See* Schiller, Richard

Song of Igor's Campaign, The, 110

Sophocles, 23, 96–97

Sopwith. *See* Lindy

Speak, Memory, 82, 110, *141–142, 144, 147–149, 150–152*

Stowe, Harriet, 23

Strange Mushroom, The, 57, 58

Style. *See* individual headings: Alliteration; Assonance; Dialogue; Double entendre; Doublets; Imagery; Lexicon; Metaphors; Names of characters; Neologisms; Puns; Rhymes; Rhythm; Similes; Synathrismus; Syntax; Transitions

Sunglasses, 42–43

Swift, Jonathan. *See* Van Ness, Vanessa

Swinburne, Algernon, 28–30, 82, *139*

Swine, 72–73

Synathrismus, 101–102
Syntax, 115–117; parenthetical non-sentence, 117

Tacitus, 89
Tigermoth. *See* Blake
Tolstoy, Leo, 89, *154; The Kreutzer Sonata,* 33
Transitions, 115–116
Trapp, Gustave, 16, 24, 68, 72–73, 99
Tristramson, Dr., 96
Turgenev, Ivan, 20

Valeria (Zborovski - Humbert), 23, 92
Van Ness, Vanessa, 96
Verlaine, Paul, 32–33, *140*
Virgil, 23
Vyazemsky, Prince, 78

Waterproof, 74–76
Who's Who in the Limelight, 58–61, 72, 77
Wine, wine, wine, 60

Zemfira and Aleko. *See* Pushkin, *The Gypsies*